This book combines two of my favorite things: personality insights and literary heroines.

ANNE BOGEL, FOUNDER OF MODERN MRS.
DARCY AND AUTHOR OF *READING PEOPLE*

Introverted Mom is a steady stream of inspiration for those of us who regularly feel depleted "keeping up" with the pace and decibel of an extroverted world. As I read Jamie's words, I felt more affirmed than I have in a long time. Seeing my own introverted tendencies as worthy traits and not "needy" quirks completely shifts the focus away from feeling not enough to celebrating the gifts that come with my personality. I wish I could set a copy of this book on the night stand of every introverted mother to remind her that understanding herself more deeply, making peace with who she is and designing her life to honor her natural traits is the greatest gift she can offer herself and her family.

LISA GRACE BYRNE, FOUNDER AND DIRECTOR
OF WELLGROUNDED LIFE

In a world that urges us to do more and be more, Jamie invites introverted moms to embrace the way God created us. With quick wit and charming literary profiles, each chapter will leave you feeling like you've just had a cup of tea with a new friend. I'm so glad Jamie had the courage to put into words the reality so many of us face on a daily basis, reminding us that we are not alone.

ASHERITAH CIUCIU, FOUNDER OF ONE THING
ALONE AND AUTHOR OF *FULL*

Jamie is a genius for taking the time to write this book. I think every woman should read it. We all want to run away and refuel on a regular basis, which is essential to emotional, spiritual and mental health. Jamie gives us permission and validation to care for ourselves. As a fellow introvert, I wish I'd had this book many years ago!

SALLY CLARKSON, AUTHOR, SPEAKER, MOTHER, AND
FELLOW INTROVERT AT SALLYCLARKSON.COM

Though I've been an introverted mom for over fifteen years, I still found myself reading Jamie's words with a highlighter in one hand and a tissue in the other. It's a relief to be reminded that my introversion is not a burden to my family, but a gift. *Introverted Mom* is a timely reminder to lean in to who we are and how we're made. I wish I'd had this book when my kids were babies!

EMILY P. FREEMAN, *WALL STREET JOURNAL* BESTSELLING AUTHOR OF *SIMPLY TUESDAY*

As a mom of six, I spent too many years following advice that didn't fit my introverted temperament. I wish I'd had Jamie Martin's book years ago! Jamie gives people like me permission to be ourselves and offers unique tips for how to thrive in our daily lives.

JENNIFER FULWILER, SiriusXM RADIO HOST AND AUTHOR OF *ONE BEAUTIFUL DREAM*

What I love most about Jamie Martin's *Introverted Mom* is her insightful encouragement to accept and embrace our own style of motherhood. We might all share the title of "Mom," but we all possess different strengths, limits, tendencies, visions and heart compositions that set us apart. This book offers tangible ways of honoring our personalities, while gaining so many of Martin's now famous how-to's on becoming our best, most authentic selves.

JESSICA KASTNER, AUTHOR OF *HIDING FROM THE KIDS IN MY PRAYER CLOSET* AND BLOGGER AT JESSICAKASTNER.COM

Creatively woven with the wisdom of classic literary cohorts, Jamie's voice in these pages offers hope for the hidden 50 percent. Finally: a motherhood anthem we introverts can dance to. (Quietly. In our bedrooms. Alone.)

ERIN LOECHNER, FOUNDER OF OTHERGOOSE .COM AND AUTHOR OF *CHASING SLOW*

I'm an extrovert, but I was delighted to discover myself in so many of this book's pages, too. We all have to both extrovert and introvert at different times, after all. Jamie's book is nourishing for the soul.

SARAH MACKENZIE, AUTHOR OF *THE READ-ALOUD FAMILY* AND CREATOR OF THE READ-ALOUD REVIVAL PODCAST

I can't tell you how many emails I have received from worn-out, introverted moms hiding in their bathrooms, the only place of brief respite in their homes. At last, Jamie Martin has written a book specifically for you, and in these pages you will begin to let go of unattainable extroverted mom ideals and find rest and strength to live and love as yourselves. Close the bathroom door, open this book, and be free!

ADAM MCHUGH, AUTHOR OF *INTROVERTS IN THE CHURCH*

Introverted Mom reminded me that introversion/extroversion is a spectrum, and that we identify with aspects of both sides at different seasons of our lives. Even though I lean toward the extroverted side of that spectrum, the loud, 24/7 role of motherhood has made me more aware than ever of my need to get away and recharge. Jamie's words showed me that I'm not alone in that need and gave me a guilt-free permission slip to care for myself.

ERIN ODOM, AUTHOR OF *MORE THAN JUST MAKING IT* AND CREATOR OF THEHUMBLEDHOMEMAKER.COM

This book is the encouragement I wish I had when my kids were younger. In these pages, Jamie manages to both lovingly remind us introverts that we're not alone in our parenting experiences, and inspire us to roll up our sleeves and do the beautiful work of raising our kids our way, leaning into the way we're made instead of fighting against it. Her voice is full of wisdom, humor, and much needed here-in-the-trenches-with-you.

TSH OXENREIDER, AUTHOR OF *AT HOME IN THE WORLD*

Parenting is hard. It requires being around people constantly; little people who are loud and messy and inquisitive without end. Their ceaseless energy has the power to weary the most outgoing, extroverted mom, and for the introverted mom this can prove crippling. *Introverted Mom* is a gift to those of us who have struggled to find a peaceful and gentle rhythm in this chaotic season of our lives.

WENDY SPEAKE, CO-AUTHOR OF *TRIGGERS*

Jamie has a beautiful way of meeting introverted moms right where they are and giving them tools for carrying on. Her encouragement throughout these pages is genuine, practical, and tangible. I felt understood and validated for who I am. What a gift. *Introverted Mom* is going to give many women a huge sigh of relief and confidence to navigate life in a way that feels authentic to them.

RACHEL MACY STAFFORD, *NEW YORK TIMES*
BESTSELLING AUTHOR OF *HANDS FREE MAMA*

After becoming a mom to an extroverted firstborn, I started to wonder if I might be an introvert, despite the fact that I am social and outgoing. Now I'm four kids into this motherhood gig, and my introverted side definitely struggles to cope! Reading *Introverted Mom* reminded me that I'm not alone in feeling overwhelmed by the joyful noises that fill my home, that needing to recharge doesn't make me a bad mom, and that there are practical steps I can take to feed my quiet-loving heart. Drawing on the wisdom of some of my favorite literary introverts, Jamie Martin's encouraging book is a balm to the soul.

HALEY STEWART, AUTHOR OF *THE GRACE OF ENOUGH*

As a mother of five and a full-time work-at-home mom, this book was nourishment for my tired spirit. Reading it was like having a (quiet) cup of tea with a friend. The pages are filled with empathy and understanding for the exhausted introvert who feels like she's not enough. *Introverted Mom* inspired me to own my strengths, and it helped me to feel less alone on my motherhood journey.

SUSAN STORM, FOUNDER OF PSYCHOLOGYJUNKIE.COM

introverted
mom

ALSO BY JAMIE C. MARTIN

Give Your Child the World

Mindset for Moms

Steady Days

introverted mom

Your Guide to More Calm, Less Guilt, and Quiet Joy

jamie c. martin

ZONDERVAN

Introverted Mom
Copyright © 2019 by Jamie C. Martin

Requests for information should be addressed to:
Zondervan, *3900 Sparks Dr. SE, Grand Rapids, Michigan 49546*

ISBN 978-0-310-35497-0 (softcover)
ISBN 978-0-310-35499-4 (audio)
ISBN 978-0-310-35498-7 (ebook)

Published in association with literary agent Jenni Burke of D.C. Jacobson & Associates LLC, an Author Management Company, www.dcjacobson.com.

Cover Design: Faceout Studio
Cover Illustrations: Creative Market
Interior design: Denise Froelich

Printed in the United States of America

19 20 21 22 23   LSC   10 9 8 7 6 5 4 3 2 1

*For my (extroverted) mom and my
(introverted) dad—the first still on earth,
the second watching from heaven: Thanks
for your unconditional love, always.*

contents

PART 1: THE TRUE WAY TO LIVE

On Discovering You're an Introverted Mom
    Retracing Childhood Clues
    Reaching the Breaking Point
    What I've Learned about Anger

On Believing That You're Enough
    Free to Be Who? On What Makes an Introvert
    Sailing Your Ship: Lessons from Louisa May Alcott
    An Introverted Mother's Promise

On the Freedom That Comes from Acceptance
    Self-Care versus Self-Improvement
    A HUGE List of True Self-Care Ideas for the
        Introverted Mom
    The Freedom of Discovering What's Yours

PART 2: GOVERNING IT WELL

On Navigating Heartache and Disappointment
    Dealing with the Tough Stuff of Life Introvert-Style
    Keeping Out the Shadows: Lessons from L. M.
        Montgomery
    Grace for the Introverted Mom

On Marriage and Raising Children
    Sparkle and Glow: On Differing Personality Types in
        Marriage
    Loud and Proud: On Raising Extroverted Children as
        an Introverted Mom
    Alone, Together: On Connecting With and Raising
        Introverts

On Stretching out of Our Comfort Zones
    Even If It's Not a Definite Yes, It Could Still Be a
        Definite Yes
    A (Hushed) Shout-Out to the Highly Sensitive
    Kneeling in the Dirt, Waiting for the Growth

PART 3: A BETTER GUIDE

PART 4: SIMPLE LITTLE PLEASURES

On Cultivating Calm Wherever You Are
    Quiet in Your World versus Quiet in Your Mind
    Living Slow: Lessons from Laura Ingalls Wilder
    A Dishwasher's Meditation

On Uncovering Joy
    Stop Trying to Be Happy and You Just Might Be
        Happier
    The Daily Checklist: A Tool for Prioritizing Positivity
    If You Give an Introverted Mom a Smartphone

On Defining for Ourselves What Really Matters
    A "Fruit-Filled" Life: A New Definition of Success
    Brave and Bad: On Being a Successful Mother
    Dear Mom of "That" Kid

you might be
an introverted
mother if . . .

If you've ever hidden a stash of chocolate
on a high shelf in the bathroom,
you might be an introverted mother.

If you occasionally need to tell someone, "Go
to your room!" and that someone is you,
you might be an introverted mother.

If you get up early or stay up late, just to soak in the silence,
you might be an introverted mother.

If you've ever begged your husband to put the
kids to bed at the end of a long day,
you might be an introverted mother.

If you know you must build in recovery
time after every playdate,
you might be an introverted mother.

If you've ever worn earplugs during time
spent with your own children,
you might be an introverted mother.

If you're secretly relieved when a
planned outing gets canceled,
you might be an introverted mother.

If you drop your child off for a lesson, and
feel lucky to sit in the car alone,
you might be an introverted mother.

If you sometimes wish you could do more, but your
body, mind, and spirit point out that you can't,
you might be an introverted mother.

If you've ever asked someone else to take
your kids to a loud birthday party,
you might be an introverted mother.

If your idea of a perfect night is a hot bath and a good book,
you might be an introverted mother.

If you've ever felt guilty about giving the kids
screen time so you can have downtime,
you might be an introverted mother.

If chitchat exhausts you, but you love meaningful
conversation with a close friend,
you might be an introverted mother.

If you've ever retreated behind your bedroom
door and cried in overwhelm,
you might be an introverted mother.

If you avoid answering the telephone
unless it's an emergency,
you might be an introverted mother.

If you've instituted a mandatory hour or
more of quiet time in the afternoons,
you might be an introverted mother.

If you consider your journal one of your
most treasured companions,
you might be an introverted mother.

If you've ever wondered why a typical
day can drain you completely,
you might be an introverted mother.

If you are compassionate, sensitive,
and love your family fiercely,
you might be an introverted mother.

If you believe a peaceful home is the best place in the world,
you might be an introverted mother.

And if you're an introverted mother, this book is for you.

Do you ever wonder if you're the only mom who feels this way? Like no one else gets you? Like the way motherhood affects you means you're just not cut out for this 24/7 role?

Come closer, because I have a secret: Your personality is no accident. In fact, you already have every trait you need to be the best unique mother for your unique kids. You may feel torn from your true self, though, because you're living in a nonstop, go-go-go society, one that constantly shouts that *louder* and *bigger* matter more. One that says you're less than if you're a caring listener and reflective thinker instead of an incessant talker and frantic doer.

This book sets the record straight. It's about letting go of Mommy Guilt we were never called to carry, about finding ways to bring in the quiet we genuinely need, about redefining and rediscovering the good life. We find ourselves in difficult times, that's for sure. Parenting in this technological age is a challenge no previous generation has faced, and staying grounded as we juggle multiple schedules and negative news feeds takes courage. But as our planet spins faster, the world and our families call out for the irreplaceable gifts that only we, as introverts, can bring. Our faith is needed. Our steadiness is needed. Our presence is needed. Our calm is needed. *We are needed.*

The details of our days differ drastically: we may work outside the home or work at home. We might homeschool or have our kids in public school. We may be called "Mom" by many or by only one. We might be unexpectedly single or have just celebrated twenty-five years of marriage. We may have biological children, have grown our family through adoption, or both, as I have. The details vary, but our introversion connects us.

Now take a moment and return to the beginning of this introduction. Count the number of "introverted mother" descriptions you identify with. Do you see yourself in ten or more? If so, welcome to the club.[1] You'll be relieved to know there aren't any loud meetings to attend. We'll just sit and read side by side, grateful that someone else finally understands. Membership lasts a lifetime, so come on in. I'm thrilled you're here.

PART 1

the true
way to live

The true way to live is to enjoy every moment

as it passes, and surely it is in the everyday

things around us that the beauty of life lies.

LAURA INGALLS WILDER,
WRITINGS FROM THE OZARKS

CHAPTER 1

the distance is nothing

ON DISCOVERING YOU'RE AN INTROVERTED MOM

I do not wish to avoid the walk. The distance is nothing when one has a motive.

JANE AUSTEN, *PRIDE AND PREJUDICE*

You're kind of a . . . homebody, aren't you?"

Her tone made it clear this was *not* a good thing.

Embarrassment colored my cheeks, but I attempted to shrug off the comment.

"Well, I don't know. Yes . . . maybe?" I answered, glancing at my new baby on a blanket nearby (thinking of how life could change so much, so fast).

GOING THE DISTANCE

I had only been a mother for a year, yet somehow I had two babies. One from my body, one from the other side of the world. Not long before this living room conversation took place, I had done the hardest thing God had asked of me up to that point. I'd kissed my one-year-old son, Jonathan, and my husband, Steve, goodbye and boarded the first of several planes on my way to a country the Department of Homeland Security had suggested Americans avoid because of its instability: Liberia, West Africa.

Before leaving, I tearfully typed Jonathan a letter to read in the future:

> Last night we found out Baby Elijah is sick with malaria, and right now he really needs a mommy with him. So I'll go for now, then come back to be Mommy to both of you. Out of all the children in the world, how could it be that I have been blessed with the best two boys of all?

After learning about Elijah's illness from the adoption agency, we scrambled to get immunizations and paperwork together to hasten my departure. My brain physically hurt trying to organize every miniscule detail. Desperately out of my element, I clung to a quote from the title my book club had recently finished: "The really wonderful moments of joy in this world are not the moments of self-satisfaction, but self-forgetfulness."[1]

Looking back, I don't know if I'd have enough courage to do now what I did then. But isn't that always the way with mothers? Somehow we dig deep, with a strength that goes far beyond our own internal resources and capabilities, to do whatever our children need. In this case, however, I didn't know the child I was sacrificing for. I hadn't even seen his picture.

Three long flights later, exhausted, I landed in another world. By that point I had joined a handful of other adoptive parents who were also coming to meet their children. An orphanage worker drove us down a dark, bumpy road to our accommodation. I'll never forget my shock the next morning when I saw it in first light: a patched-up concrete shelter that looked barely held together.

I'd shortly find myself barely holding together as well.

Twenty minutes after I held my six-month-old son, tears flowing with a mix of joy, awe, stress, and jet lag, Elijah vomited on me. Then he did it again. And again. During our first endless night together, I kept vigil beside this sick, small stranger, wondering if I had a dying child beside me. The next morning we drove to the US embassy, then the nearest hospital: the care basic, the wait eternal. After four hours, a doctor finally told me that Elijah's best chance for survival was to get to the United States ASAP.

Recalling the forty-eight-hour journey to Liberia, I didn't think I could physically make the return trip so soon. I had only slept a handful of hours since I'd arrived in West Africa. God put an angel in my path, though, a missionary who offered to watch my son through the night so I could rest.

"Thank you so much, but I don't think I would feel comfortable leaving him all night," I said. "Maybe I could just take a nap and then come get him?"

More than eight hours later, I woke, stunned to realize how much time had passed. I raced to Elijah, murmured my heartfelt thanks to the man who had watched over him, and prepared to head back to the airport. Years and fatigue have mostly blurred the two-day journey home, but there's one part I'll never forget.

At the Brussels airport, I realized we were in serious danger of missing our flight. Boarding ended in twenty minutes, and the security line stretched to an hour's wait or more. Desperate mothers—no matter their personality type—do desperate things, don't we? Without a second thought, I ran to the front, passing more than a hundred people. Heart pounding, with Elijah in a Baby Bjorn strapped to my chest, I said to the man standing there, "Sir, our flight leaves in a few minutes, and I'm trying to get this sick baby home. Please can we go next?"

He looked at the handful of people around him, at the long line curving behind in the distance. Glancing back at me, he spoke words I'll always remember: "Well, now, I don't see how anyone could argue with that."

Gratitude overcame me, and an instant later I bolted through the terminal, my baby's head bobbing up and down as I ran all the way to the gate. We just made it. I sat down in our seat, sweaty from the stress and exertion, wanting to sob but lacking the energy. I willed myself to do what had to be done in the days and weeks ahead as our family pursued every avenue available to keep Elijah alive. It worked.

In case you're feeling at all impressed with me by this point, don't be. When the immediate danger had finally passed, the tension, pent-up fear, and yes, the tears, all caught up with me. Like maybe they'd never stop. Like maybe I'd never get back to "myself." Whoever I was. In this new mothering role, I had no clue.

All of these experiences flashed through my mind in an instant as I stood in my living room, accused of being a homebody. How could I possibly qualify for that label with all we'd just gone through? And even if I did, why would it be a bad thing?

I had crisscrossed the globe on this crazy adventure, much of it on my own. Yet somehow, when I walked into our local moms' group, which rotated houses each week, my head began to swirl. A dozen cute kids ran from one end of the room to the other in all their noisy glory. Mothers tried to keep them safe and happy while also attempting to get in a sentence of conversation here and there.

After my first visit, I had to rest on the couch for a couple of hours. After my second, I decided I'd rather just meet up with the moms one-on-one instead of attend a group playdate. But the other women seemed to enjoy the large, loud gathering.

How could I travel the world, yet be unable to handle the noise down the street?

What is wrong with me? I wondered. And not for the first time.

RETRACING CHILDHOOD CLUES

Maybe you were the girl who climbed a tree to gain distance and a new perspective. Or maybe, while the other kids screamed in fun during dodgeball, you'd lean *toward* the ball, get knocked out early, and have an excuse to sit on the bench before heading back to class. Maybe you hung out at the library instead of the mall. Perhaps you noticed some of these signs; perhaps you didn't. But clues pointing to your introversion have always been there.

In my case, I turned my closet into a private childhood getaway, long before tiny houses became fashionable. As if my small bedroom wasn't snug enough. An avid bookworm, I found more than enough adventure between the covers of a book and my imagination. I retreated to the television before tackling my homework, desperate to escape for a few hours after being surrounded by people all day. I was the good girl who couldn't make her needs known too loudly, the one who tried to follow the rules. If I could just follow all the rules, I could prove to myself that I mattered. Instead of turning to the social scene for affirmation, as an extrovert might have, I turned to the inner world of academics, "making the grade" in an attempt to earn my worth. But of course, it was never enough.

How I wish I could have known this truth from Susan Cain, author of the bestseller *Quiet: The Power of Introverts in a World That Can't Stop Talking*: "Being introverted is not something to outgrow; it is something to accept and grow into—and even to cherish."[2] I've spent more than three decades attempting to "accept and grow into" myself, but only in the past handful of years have I ventured to take a few tentative steps on the "cherishing" path. Once I dared to do so, I discovered flowers blooming alongside it, giddy joy among its quiet twists and turns.

I took my first personality test in high school, at age fourteen. No doubt the intent was to offer teens vocational advice as we began to consider our futures. I pondered the results during Civics class from my desk at the back of the room. The test seemed like a game, the kind my friends and I used to play with folded paper to figure out who our husband would be and where we'd live someday. I read my description as if visiting a career counselor / fortune-teller, laughing aloud when the job portion of the results suggested I train horses for a living, since I wasn't an animal person and had no experience around equines. The jumble of letters, tagging me as an "INFJ," didn't mean much—except that I noticed the "I" stood for "introversion." Having read about the differences between extroverts and introverts already, I knew on some level that society preferred the first. Though I'm not sure I could have articulated it, that "I" brought back a little embarrassment and a few memories.

I remembered how in the sixth grade, I asked my beloved teacher, Mrs. Wright, if I could move my desk away from the other kids and up by hers "so I could have more quiet." I recalled how it touched my heart when she said yes, how grown up I felt when I pushed my fake wooden desk with the shiny metal legs over to face hers. How I felt a little less overwhelmed by the school days that followed.

I thought about how even now, after a full day of high school, I watched other kids head off to part-time jobs or friends' houses. That rarely appealed to me, though, so I'd usually find myself heading home to recharge for a few hours before starting my homework, heading to youth group, or attending choir practice. "Why don't you have a friend over or go out?" Dad sometimes asked. And I did: restaurants, movies, football games. But every time the question came up, I had to wonder, *What is wrong with me?* As I held the personality profile in my hands, I suspected this mysterious "I" could be to blame.

Over the years I learned to manage my introversion. If I had an extremely draining day, another came along that allowed me to rest. College, marriage, and then a full-time job made this more challenging to do, but I could still control and regulate my environment to some degree. Then came motherhood, bringing with it joy and love like I'd never known—as well as sleep deprivation, no days off, and constant needs to meet. Eventually, it also brought me to a breaking point.

REACHING THE BREAKING POINT

The glass left my hand and slammed into the wall on the far side of the bedroom, shattering into hundreds of shards on the carpet. As I turned to the side, I caught a glimpse of my reflection in the mirror before sinking to the ground in sobs. I didn't recognize myself.

I had managed fairly well as an introverted mom with just one child to care for. I had time to rest during Jonathan's naps and, after he began sleeping through the night, long evenings to spend alone with Steve. Even sleep deprivation was almost endurable with just one baby. But when Elijah came home at death's door, my margin dissipated and my stress levels rose. And two years later, when we adopted our daughter, Trishna, from India at the age of four, the reality of having three little ones less than two years apart in age hit me hard.

Of course, like we all do when we're insecure, I compared myself to other moms. I saw mothers in my neighborhood heading off to jobs, juggling daycare as well as volunteering with what seemed to be ease. I saw other stay-at-home moms crafting with their kids, cooking their families' food from scratch, and refusing to use screen time to occupy their kids no matter what. Somehow, even as I tried to give my best to my family, I couldn't shake the feeling that I was failing.

It wasn't that I didn't love my children. It wasn't that I didn't want to care for them. I had been called to and *wanted* to do both of those things. They had been my dreams. But as an introverted mother, the sudden increase in noise and in chaos kept my nervous system in overdrive every day. I didn't understand that at the time, though. That outburst with the glass happened over ten years ago, thankfully without anyone present, but I'll never forget it. I realized I could no longer continue just getting by. I could no longer ignore the warning signs.

What is wrong with me? Why can't I do this? I wondered.

Not long ago, I came across a list of the major factors that stress out my particular personality type on the blog Psychology Junkie. I had to laugh (or cry) when I realized that nearly all of them appear repeatedly in a mom's daily life! Can you relate?

Introverted Stressors (with my own notes added as they relate to motherhood):

- Having to focus too much on sensory / concrete details (*"Mom, what's for breakfast, lunch, dinner?!"*)
- An overload of sensory stimulation or noise (*Um, hello, children!*)
- Interruptions (*Like I said.*)
- Distress within close relationships (*All. the. time.*)
- Having values violated (*Wanting to change the world, but changing diapers instead.*)
- Not enough alone time; too much extroverting (*Hmm, just a tad.*)
- Working with closed-minded people (*Oh, of course you're having a tantrum because your toothbrush is blue, not red!*)
- Not receiving appreciation or understanding (*Here's looking at you, kid.*)
- Unfamiliar environments with excessive amounts of details (*Sounds like a group playdate.*)
- Having plans disrupted (*Part of the job description, right?*)
- Not having a clear direction (*But somehow I'm the one in charge!*)
- Lack of harmony (*Sibling drama, anyone?*)

- Criticism and conflict (*Rinse and repeat.*)
- Not being able to use intuition or envision the future
  (*Yep, no idea how this experiment will turn out.*)
- Having to focus too much on the present (*All day, every day.*)

"When under stress," the article went on, my type "may become uncharacteristically angry and quick-tempered, unreasonable, and irrational."[3] Yeah, you got me. They might as well have added, "may begin to throw breakable objects at any time."

What I've Learned about Anger

I never thought of myself as an angry person until I had kids. Ever. I don't think anyone else would have used that adjective to describe me either. A former boss thought me so calm, she always wanted me nearby in stressful moments. As a young mom, however, I didn't understand enough about my personality to make sense of the transition I was undergoing as an introvert. But throughout the past decade of parenting life, I've learned three truths about anger that comfort me.

Anger is the natural response to the hard parts of motherhood, especially as an introvert.

For years, a pleasant, magical mother lived in my head, taunting me. She never got angry, but responded to her children in a sing-song voice like this:

"Oh, you bit your brother again? Don't do that, sweetie!" (spoken while gathering the child in a hug).

"You threw your toys all over the room during a tantrum and broke a window? We're both going to laugh about this someday!"

"You didn't like any of your birthday presents? I'm sorry. What else can we get you?"

Realizing that anger is the *natural* response to these situations— and that anger in itself is not wrong—lifted a huge weight of guilt off my shoulders.

Anger is an indicator to pause or change something.

Comparing anger to hunger helps. After all, we don't try to eliminate hunger from our lives. It's just a cue, a signal that our body needs fuel. Anger is also a cue from our body, a signal that we need to pause.

We don't just "press through" for the sake of it. We change course, walk away, breathe before dealing with the situation. Anger points the way toward peace if we pay attention.

Quiet is a must for an introverted mom.

Our kids cannot flourish in our homes if we constantly live on the edge of our God-given personalities. We are all connected within these walls. That means we must do whatever we can to recharge on a daily basis.

We can lament this fact or view it as a gift. Regardless, it is a necessity, and if we neglect it, every person in our home will pay the price. By taking care of ourselves, we can care for others well. This, after all, is what we most long to do.

OUR MOTIVE AND WHY IT MATTERS

The desire to care for our families well is why we gather over these pages. As Jane Austen said, "The distance is nothing when one has a motive," and boy, do we have one. Maybe our motive has a sweet grin and a few teeth missing. Maybe he has never-ending energy and gives slippery kisses. Maybe she looks up from her crib with arms stretched toward you, the most important person in her universe.

We aren't attempting to make our lives calmer out of self-ishness. We are mothers, called to lay down our very lives for our children if necessary. We are here because our families deserve our best. Because we deserve to understand ourselves, our strengths *and* weaknesses. There's nothing wrong with you, fellow introverted mom. And I hope that by the time you finish this book, you will have begun to believe that.

I write these words not because I'm an expert, but because I needed this book and it didn't exist. How I desperately needed this book! I needed someone to confirm that there was nothing fundamentally flawed with the mother I was. That my instincts could be trusted. That I wasn't ruining my children. That some-how my family could live together without me constantly feeling like I was at the end of my rope. I offer these words in the hope that other introverted mothers will come by these insights more easily and earlier than I did.

I share mainly through stories because that's how I've always learned best. If it ever sounds like I love to talk about myself, know that like many introverts, I'm a private person. I aim to share vulnerably, though, with permission from my loved ones, so that you'll know you aren't alone. If I ever come across like I know what I'm doing in these stories, rest assured that this is a figment of your imagination. If I come across like a mess held together by mercy, you're nearer the right track. And at the end of the chapters coming up, I offer "Reflections for Introverted Moms" for you—short sections of poetry, encouragement, or humor—because, let's face it, when it comes to motherhood, practical suggestions only take us so far. We need laughter, tears, and inspiration, just as much (if not more) than we need helpful advice. But these aren't solely my own thoughts scribbled on these pages. I offer yours, too, given here and there in bite-sized snippets of wisdom from the places you've shared them: blog comments, social media, emails. Not on the phone, though, because, hello: We're introverts, remember?

I've also invited some of my dearest friends to travel this introverted journey with us. In the interest of full disclosure, I don't actually know them and they all happen to be dead, but if they were still alive—I know they would *love* me. We'd be besties, sitting quietly together drinking hot tea, eating cookies, and reading books. Four of my favorite writers, all introverted women themselves, will walk beside us: Louisa May Alcott, Jane Austen, L. M. Montgomery, and Laura Ingalls Wilder. Their words have inspired me since I first met each one of them, long before I knew we all shared the gift of introversion. I've pulled all the chapter titles in this book from their writings, and throughout these pages we'll touch base with them to glean insights from their lives that still apply to us today.

"Why does any of this even matter?" you might ask. Well, if you're an introverted mother, it matters because it's part of the woman you are. Part of the girl you once were. A part that maybe you didn't understand, that maybe no one understood. A part that perhaps you still haven't come to terms with. An introverted renaissance has ignited our society in recent years. Word has gotten out, finally, that introversion isn't a mistake or a weakness. That this personality trait allows those who possess it to thrive and find purpose. That someone's desire for quiet isn't wrong, but instead what they truly need in order to be able to offer their gifts to others.

And yet I've continued to wonder: How does this apply to motherhood? I don't know about you, but my kids didn't get the memo that they should try to accommodate my personality type. The common advice to "just take care of yourself" as an introvert doesn't come easily to those of us in this 24/7 role. We have a challenge on our hands, which is why we need this book. Together we're going to pioneer an introverted motherhood revolution, helping our families, touching the world, and if we're lucky, maybe even scoring fifteen minutes alone here and there along the way.

Reflections from Introverted Moms

HOW DID YOU FIRST DISCOVER YOU WERE AN INTROVERTED MOM?

I think it became blatant when we got home from an extended family event and I was utterly overwhelmed. These were people I dearly loved and enjoyed, but I sat down and cried afterward because it was too much. I started saying no to big gatherings, getting together with my extended family in smaller visits instead. That has actually worked . . . because I've been blessed to get to know them better.

TALIA, ILLINOIS

It probably wasn't until my daughter was three, when I started to get drained by all the talking, questioning, and noise that came with motherhood.

TIFFANY, CANADA

I first started seeing my introversion affect my parenting when my extroverted daughter wanted to invite neighbor kids over to our house all the time. I could feel my anxiety levels rising! We had to come up with some boundaries about when friends were allowed over, for how long, and how many at a time.

BRENDA, MINNESOTA

I never knew I was an introvert until I became a mother. At the end of every day, during which my two young children had been with me every waking second, all I could think about was handing them off to my husband and taking a book and a glass of wine up to the bathtub.

MICHELLE, INDIANA

I knew [I was an introvert] before the kids, but having them attached to me all the time gets overwhelming. Nap time is Me Time.

BROOKE, COLORADO

CHAPTER 2

learning how to sail

✦

ON BELIEVING THAT YOU'RE ENOUGH

I'm not afraid of storms, for I'm learning how to sail my ship.

LOUISA MAY ALCOTT, *LITTLE WOMEN*

Mommy, sometimes do you not want to be with me? Because sometimes I feel like you don't want me with you."

The little voice rose up beside me on the brown leather sofa, at the end of a looooonnnng day that still wasn't over. I looked down into the wide eyes of my son Jonathan, feeling like I'd been punched in the stomach. All my failures rushed over me—all the things I wished I could be but wasn't. All the energy and patience

I wanted but didn't have. With childlike wisdom and bluntness, he saw the truth and spoke it.

And it *was* the truth: I didn't want him with me.

What kind of mother admits that? The desperate, introverted kind, whose husband left several days ago on a work trip. The kind who's settled countless sibling squabbles, made countless meals, read countless books, and counted down countless hours until bedtime's arrival. The kind who's just been completely called out by a nine-year-old as she's nearing that glorious home stretch.

I knew all about an introvert's strengths and weaknesses, knew the theoretical reasons why I felt exhausted and drained, but none of that mattered. My little boy felt unwanted, and it crushed me. I blundered for a few minutes, reminded him about the difference between introverts and extroverts, prayed with him, then watched as he scampered upstairs—looking for all intents and purposes like he hadn't been scarred for life. I thought *I* might be, though. While the kids drifted off to a full night's sleep, I tossed and turned for hours, wrestling my inner demons and my own nature, which once again seemed inadequate.

On Plenty in Weakness

Not enough: this fearful refrain tormented me that night. I had given the kids my best during the challenging day prior to Jonathan's bedtime declaration. Yet he still felt it was lacking. When the stress of real life comes our way, it won't be perfection we offer our kids, but it's our best all the same. What more can we do?

My friend Lisa Grace Byrne, an inspiring writer, teacher, and mama-encourager, describes it like this: In certain seasons of our mothering life, it's as though we walk through a flat, grassy field.

The terrain is smooth and comfortable; the scenery lovely. We cover a lot of ground that way, making measurable progress one step at a time. But then we reach the edge of the meadow and find a steep rock wall towering in front of us. Turning around and going back isn't an option, and the only way to continue moving forward is to climb—one slow, shaky grip and foothold after another. It's still progress, of course, but it looks nothing like the open countryside. The best we can offer our families in the meadows of life differs wildly from the best we bring when we're scaling walls—when Daddy gets deployed, when the doctor delivers a scary diagnosis, or when we've once again reached the end of our reserves.

I finally understood this on a deeper level with a life coach's help, when I mentioned to her that my mind rang with "not enough" loudly and on repeat. She sent me on a hunt for a Scripture I could use to combat this lie. I landed on Paul's words in 2 Corinthians 12:7–9: "I was given a thorn in my flesh, a messenger from Satan to torment me and keep me from becoming proud. Three different times I begged the Lord to take it away. Each time he said, 'My grace is all you need. My power works best in weakness.' So now I am glad to boast about my weaknesses, so that the power of Christ can work through me" (NLT).

I had read this Scripture dozens of times, but now a new meaning jumped out. If God's power works best in weakness, it's better to have weaknesses! Better to be "not enough," because then he can work without me getting in the way. Suddenly I saw this verse as an equation that literally adds up to enough for those in my home:

God's Grace + My Weakness = ENOUGH

It's my new life mantra; the one I repeat to myself when, again, my best isn't *the* best. When I'm drained, overwhelmed, and "don't want them with me." Can you get a hold on the freedom found here, fellow introverted mom? It means that even your biggest failures and shortcomings can be used by God, transformed via his miraculous alchemy into gold that enriches your family. It means you are free.

FREE TO BE WHO? ON WHAT MAKES AN INTROVERT

The kids ran down the porch steps, eager to get to a much-anticipated summer camp. As they climbed into the van, I reminded one of my sons that when he returned, he'd need to have some "introvert time"—a phrase we use to denote playing or reading alone. We've learned the hard way that when he tries to continue being around people nonstop after a morning of extroverting, it doesn't end well. He needs me to step in and make sure he gets that quiet. If only we introverted mothers had someone to do the same for us!

"I don't need that; I *like* people," my extroverted daughter said as she buckled her seat belt.

"Yeah, me too," Jonathan, another extrovert, chimed in.

"Guys, I also like people and so does Elijah," I reminded them. "That's not what being an introvert means."

Where do they pick up these stereotypes? I asked myself. Then I did my best to once again describe introversion in language we could all understand. The difference between extroverts and introverts boils down mainly to one thing: ENERGY, both where and how we get it. Think of an electrical device, like your mobile phone. When it needs recharging, you plug it in. Simple! Now let's imagine that the current running through the outlet represents time spent with people, and *you* are the device. Extroverts plug themselves in, heading to their events, meetings, groups, or even just a regular day after a good night's sleep. Of course they'll have challenges and face difficult moments like anyone, but if they can stay plugged in to situations, people, and conversations they love, they'll thrive, all thanks to that highly-charged energy.

But not all electrical currents are the same. I learned this the hard way when I went to London during spring break as a college freshman. I may have been in pursuit of a cute British boy who became my husband a few years later, and as such, I had all my glamorous accessories with me. That first day I sported bright white tights beneath a denim miniskirt. A long-sleeved red shirt made of felt completed my well-chosen ensemble. I was rocking it, and any young man would have been nuts not to fall for me!

As a seasoned global traveler, I knew I couldn't plug my 110-volt hair dryer straight into the 220-volt outlet in my hotel. I needed an adapter to do so, and I had come prepared. After settling in with my university group, I took a shower, plugged in my hair dryer, and started to style my hair. The dryer turned on with a strong hum, but soon the noise changed to something more akin to the sound of a loud, injured cow. A burning smell filled the bathroom, and suddenly the dryer died completely. What? Why? Then I remembered: although I technically *could* plug it into the wall, thanks to my adapter, I had neglected to bring a converter to change the electricity into a current that would not damage my equipment. That strong current was simply too much for my tool and IT BURNED OUT. Spoiler alert: Steve still married me, despite what my hair looked like and despite the white tights, decidedly uncool even back then.

See where I'm going with this, introverted mums (that's a nod to my British readers, who are always so patient with my

Americanisms)? Plugging ourselves into a highly charged current drains us rather than restores us. We *love* people: our families, friends, neighbors, coworkers, as well as those we meet at churches, groups, and activities—so much so that at times we may even be mistaken for extroverts. And if we've started our day with a fully charged battery, we will be good to go—for a while. But eventually we will run down. We have to disconnect ourselves and unplug, metaphorically but likely literally as well, to regain our energy. Time alone is our converter. And that's no small challenge for mothers because pulling the plug, so to speak, is not simple when we're constantly surrounded by little people.

Dictionary.com defines an introvert as "a person concerned primarily with *(and therefore recharged by)* his or her own thoughts and feelings rather than with the external environment." By contrast, an extrovert is "a person concerned primarily with *(and therefore recharged by)* the physical and social environment." *(My additions in italics.)* Does the idea of being "concerned primarily with your own thoughts and feelings" sound selfish? Think of it this way instead: As introverted moms, we spend much of our time meeting the needs of others. Because we're internal rather than external processors, it makes perfect sense that we need quiet with our inner selves to process and sort through our day, in order to gear up for the next one.

Of course, definitions of introversion abound and include many characteristics. Author Susan Cain mentions traits like needing less stimulation to function well, working slowly and deliberately on one task at a time, and preferring to give our social energies to close friends and family. In her words, introverts also tend to "listen more than they talk, think before they speak, and often feel as if they express themselves better in writing than in conversation."[1] Hand raised here! Thank God that the world is populated not only with people who constantly fill its airwaves, but also with those who find meaning in it all. We introverts take our thoughtful insights and offer them back to our families and others as gifts that would never exist otherwise. Let's take a look at one introverted woman who did just that and see what we can learn from her.

SAILING YOUR SHIP: LESSONS FROM LOUISA MAY ALCOTT

Niles, partner of Roberts, asked me to write a girls' book. Said I'd try. F. asked me to be the editor of "Merry's Museum." Said I'd try. Began at once on both new jobs; but didn't like either.

SEPTEMBER 1867 (AGE 35)

Louisa May Alcott's ship came in after a publisher suggested she write a novel for girls. The resulting *Little Women* took the world by storm in 1868, as her story of the four March sisters and their family captivated the hearts of young and old, completely reversing the Alcotts' financial fortune in the process. Just as her book's character Josephine imagines, Louisa (1832–88) used her earnings to fix up the family home, making their large brown house in Concord, Massachusetts, more comfortable for real-life sisters Anna, Beth, and May, as well as for Father and their mother, Marmee.

The brown house still stands in Concord, surrounded by literary greatness on every side: Nathaniel Hawthorne's family next door, Ralph Waldo Emerson down the street, Henry David Thoreau's Walden Pond within walking distance. When you stroll up to Orchard House, so named for the forty apple trees out back, you can't help but reflect on the insights that came together in this one town. Was it something in the water? Purely divine inspiration? Doesn't it sound dreamy to move from poverty and obscurity to riches and fame within the course of one year? Ah, but we know there's more to it. Because once your ship comes in, you have to learn to sail it, through both smooth and stormy seas.

Growing up, introverted Louisa found herself in an atmosphere of deep thoughts and strong ideals. As a philosopher and educator, her father's beliefs about engaging children through learning put him far ahead of his time. Most people weren't ready to embrace his concepts. Bronson Alcott started schools nearly everywhere the family moved, and all of them failed, leaving the family in dire financial straits. His thoughts about educating girls were seen as equally radical, and the neighborhood couldn't believe it when he built Louisa her own desk to support her writing efforts. That white desk remains in the second story of the house today, centered between the two front windows of Louisa's room, perfect for looking down over the street below.

> *We had lessons each morning in the study. And very*
> *happy hours they were to us, for my father taught*
> *in the wise way which unfolds what lies in the child's*
> *nature, as a flower blooms, rather than crammed it,*
> *like a Strasburg goose, with more than it could digest.*[2]

Though the neighbors knew Louisa as a gifted storyteller—it's said that people would sometimes stop by just to hear her describe an ordinary day—as an introvert she found ways to let those she loved know what she needed and when. Close friends and family members knew to check the position of her "mood pillow" on the sofa to see what to expect. If she had it propped vertically, leaning up against the sofa's arm, it meant you could engage her in a chat. But if you saw it placed horizontally, it meant she needed quiet. Amazing! I think introverted mothers everywhere need a mood pillow of their own, some way to let our family and friends know what we need in any given moment. The tricky part would be getting our littles to notice and follow its signals, right?

Fame didn't come naturally to Louisa, who struggled with becoming a public figure. On one hand, she loved that her family benefited from her writing efforts, and she adored the readers who made that happen. On the other, she felt the need to escape the attention at times. Perhaps this is why, when adoring fans would come knocking on her door, she sometimes answered with a foreign accent, pretending to be the maid.

> *I get very little time to write or think; for my working days have begun, and when (teaching) school is over Anna wants me; so I have no quiet. I think a little solitude every day is good for me. In the quiet I see my faults, and try to mend them; but, deary me, I don't get on at all.*

> AUGUST 1850 (AGE 17)

Personality gurus think that Louisa May Alcott may fit into the Myers-Briggs personality type indicator as an ISFJ, the introverted personality type referred to as the Protector, "ready to defend loved ones" at any time.[3] This seems likely, given that Louisa's motivation for her work stemmed not only from a desire to express her creativity and talent, but also from her fierce commitment to family and the responsibility she felt to help reverse their financial situation.

Toward the end of *Little Women*, one grown sister remarks to another, "I'm not afraid of storms, for I'm learning how to sail my ship."[4] For an introvert, it doesn't take much effort to sail when the sun is out, the wind still, the water smooth. But as moms, we know that family life regularly rocks our boats. Occasionally we hit our stride and miraculously, all our family members seem to be in a steady place. We exhale into the calm. An hour (or a minute) later, chaos flares once more and we're reminded that when it comes to children, regular storms go with the territory.

> *I can imagine an easier life, but with love, health,*
> *and work I can be happy; for these three help one to*
> *do, to be, and to endure all things.*

FEBRUARY 28, 1868 (AGE 35)

Yet the very storms we fight against can be a blessing if we let their winds steer us in a new direction. I remember one period when the limited television time I allow my kids each day turned into a problem, with arguments between them all but ruining it. I counted on this quiet and found its interruption deeply discouraging. In thinking through the situation, however, I realized that one of my children needed more time alone. We worked out a system wherein he could play outside while his siblings watched their video, then they would switch and he'd watch the same video while his siblings played outside. Voila! Suddenly I ended up with double the amount of time to myself. A small thing, yes, but a huge mothering win, all because I let myself drift with the storm instead of pushing against it.

Introverted Mom Takeaways from the Alcotts' Family Life

Find support.

I love the way the Alcott family, through ups, downs, and imperfections, supported one another's efforts. It's an atmosphere I long to create in our home. We're also fortunate these days that we can look for the support we need online. I have met true friends in online spaces: by connecting via social media (in my case homeschooling-related groups) and by following the blogs of like-minded women. Find a few people who "get" you and understand your personality; luckily, as an introvert, you only need a few!

Let your kids be themselves.

I wonder if the four Alcott girls, each one an artist in her own way, cultivated their talents so well because of their father's progressive ideas and their mother's unconditional love. Even as we teach our children to understand us as introverts, let's work to accept them for who they are. In our family this has led us to search for activities that fit each child's gifts and needs, whether horseback riding or nature school, online drawing classes or book discussion groups.

Look for a creative outlet.

Creativity is not exclusive to hobbies like drawing and painting—it includes gardening, cooking, reading for pleasure, journal writing, and more. A creative outlet boosts our mental health and our ability to keep going as introverted mothers. I couldn't make it through a day without a chapter of fiction and at least a quick note—if not a full brain dump—in my journal.

Show your family what you need.

Mood pillows, anyone? As your children get older, teach them signals for times when you simply must have a break from talking or listening. My go-to phrase is "Mommy's feeling a little overwhelmed right now and needs quiet." Another introverted mom told me her signal is to put her face in her hands and pray; her kids have learned this means they need to calm down fast!

Movement and fresh air.

In spite of the behavioral expectations placed on women during her time, Louisa loved to run. She scandalized the neighborhood yet again (Oh, Louisa!) by getting up early to do so outside. Later it was discovered that Louisa had mercury poisoning in her blood from medicine she took during the Civil War. Because of her active lifestyle, she lived much longer than she would have otherwise. Can you fit a tiny bit of guilt-free movement or fresh air into your current routine? During especially busy times, I make it a goal to get outside and take a walk around the yard, even if that is all I can manage.

A Room of Her Own.

Louisa's light and airy room on the upper level of Orchard House overflows with inspiration: her treasured books, her sister May's art on the walls, her writing projects. All introverted women need a space, even if just a small corner, to call their own. I adore my antique writing desk in the corner of our bedroom, with its citrus candle and a coaster for a cup of tea always at the ready.

WANT TO LEARN MORE ABOUT LOUISA? CHECK OUT:

- Her most popular / well-known piece: *Little Women* (originally published in two parts in 1868/69, when she was thirty-six)
- The first full-length novel she had published: *Moods* (published in 1864, when she was thirty-two)
- Something a little different: *A Long Fatal Love Chase* (considered "too sensational" to be seen in print during her lifetime, this thriller shot onto *The New York Times* Best Seller list when it was finally published in 1996)
- Her own candid thoughts: *The Journals of Louisa May Alcott*, edited by Joel Myerson and Daniel Shealy

REFLECTIONS FOR INTROVERTED MOMS

An Introverted Mother's Promise

"Mommy, don't you want me with you?"
a little voice asks the question.
My heart sinks, knowing the answer.

Dear babe of mine, I can't promise
constant companionship
or around-the-clock playtimes.

I can't promise that I'll never shush
or ask you to calm down,
that I won't cry in complete overwhelm.

But I can promise this, my child:

I will love you with a soft, fierce loyalty.
One that will never desert or give up,
just as He has loved and promised us both.

Great pain brought you into the world,
and when pain invades your world again,
I will go through that with you, too.

My steady faithfulness is yours for life,
like it or not—
and sometimes you won't.

Because introverted moms hold a secret:

An inner mama bear, ready to fight and defend.
You might not think I have it in me,
but I'll rile up the instant you're threatened.

My steadfast prayers will follow you
all the days of my life,
and continue into eternity.

So the answer is yes, my love,
I *do* want you with me.
Forever and always.

But can Mommy just go to the bathroom alone, please?

Reflections from Introverted Moms

❧━•••○○•••━❧

WHAT DOES BEING AN INTROVERT MEAN TO YOU? HOW WOULD YOU DEFINE IT?

For me, being introverted has less to do with being around people and more to do with having enough "space" for myself. When my daily life is calm and the rhythm is quiet, I can fully explore my own ideas and thoughts, which refreshes me and feeds my soul. I am then happy to be around others and may even find the time life-giving. But if life around me has been too chaotic, disjointed, or demanding, I struggle to find joy in socializing with other people, and it drains me simply because I feel like I had nothing to give to the interactions in the first place.

BRIANNA, WISCONSIN

I used to see it as something wrong with me, something to be "gotten over" . . . since I know so many extroverts and I always seem to be the different one. But since I accepted it wasn't a personality flaw and I was made this way for a reason, I started viewing it as having the knowledge to better care for myself.

ANDIE, TURKEY

While times around certain people drain me, being around people with whom I am comfortable and can have deep conversations recharges me. I have found that it's not the people I am around who drain me but the small talk! A part I love about being introverted is the introspective aspect. I am able to take my introspective approach to life and apply it to my children's lives. It helps me to be more in tune with their needs.

BECKY, WYOMING

Being introverted means processing internally and alone, where my thoughts aren't distracted by people or events. Don't ask me a question and expect an immediate answer. I need to process away from everyone and everything. And when there's a lot going on and a lot to process, I have to get away from it all to settle my brain.

MELEA, CALIFORNIA

Being an introvert means living a somewhat structured but low-key life. Being in a social setting zaps my energy. I have to mentally prepare just for church on Sundays and Wednesdays. I often need quiet time alone to gather my thoughts and have peace. My children are fairly outgoing, but I hope I can instill in them the need for quiet time and reflection. It's hard to hear God with so much noise in the background.

KELLEY, FLORIDA

CHAPTER 3

a new day

ON THE FREEDOM THAT
COMES FROM ACCEPTANCE

Isn't it nice to think that tomorrow is a new day
with no mistakes in it yet?

L. M. MONTGOMERY, *ANNE OF GREEN GABLES*

We have someone to help with the kids now, so why do I *still* feel drained and exhausted?"

When Steve and I decided to adopt a four-year-old from India, our beautiful daughter Trishna, we agreed we'd need extra support. After all, taking care of Jonathan and Elijah, both still toddlers, already pushed me to my limits most days. Adding another child to the mix seemed nuts, yet I knew that God has a track record of calling his people to the crazy. Several months after Elijah entered our lives and regained his health, we began to hope for another child. Through our adoption agency we found out about Trishna, and after much prayer, we began the lengthy process. The day we received the phone call, during our first family vacation, saying that the agency had approved us as her parents was one of the happiest moments of my life as a mother. But I knew there was no way I could physically, emotionally, or mentally handle a third child without help. We had three problems, however, when it came to getting that help: no extra money, no family nearby, and I could only imagine one person I'd trust enough to invite into our growing tribe.

"It would have to be someone like Sarah," I said to Steve. We had met Sarah years earlier when we both worked full-time with the organization Mercy Ships. Kind and gentle, she had been one of the first people to meet each of our boys after they joined our family. But now we lived thousands of miles away in Connecticut. I began to pray we could miraculously find someone with the same heart for children that she had.

Then God surpassed my wildest expectations. Not long after I started praying about this, I received an email from Sarah herself: "I got into grad school in New Haven," she wrote, "so I'll be moving there for two years!" Chills came over me as I sensed God's presence and saw that once again, he had shown up and done something incredible. In faith we asked Sarah to help us around eight hours a week, trusting that if God had provided the right person, he would also provide the money. Somehow he always did.

Soon our family of four became a family of five, and we began trying to parent our tiny brood, including our newest addition, who had never been parented before. Steve stayed home for a while as we adjusted to this new life, and Sarah became an invaluable help, especially when he had to go back to work. We divided her hours between two days of the week. I clung to "Sarah days" like a drowning person to a life preserver, grateful for the extra pair of hands to help with my four-, three-, and two-year-olds. Since their ages created an instant preschool in our home, and since the days could be so long (I didn't know yet if the years were short; they felt long, too), I did my best to set up a preschool routine for us: story time, music time, outside time, art time, mealtime, and so on.

Remember the movie *About a Boy*? Hugh Grant's character, a young man who doesn't have to work for a living, finds he must divide his day into "units" of fifteen-minute segments so it doesn't feel overwhelming and interminable. That was life with three energetic preschoolers:

Story Time: 1 unit (on a good day maybe 2!)
Music Time: 1 unit (then it took me 2 units to recover
   from the kazoo and tambourine usage)
Outside Time: 2 or even 3 units if we walked to the park
   around the corner—yes!
Art Time: 1 unit (and another unit spent wondering why
   finger painting was ever invented
Video Time: An episode of *Little Einsteins* so I could sit
   down, regroup, or clean, 2 units

Without a flexible plan, the hours, days, weeks, months, and years stretched endlessly ahead. But with God's assistance—and Sarah's!—I could cope. Yet I made a critical error, one I might have seen coming if I had understood my personality better. As a result, I soon found myself just as drained as before, despite Sarah's help.

I used Sarah as my "preschool assistant"—someone to help with arts and crafts, deal with messes, fix meals, or handle two kids while I dealt with a third's screams. Having another person around definitely helped, but it did not give me what I needed most: elusive, precious time to recharge. After a few months, I figured out I had to be alone to make Sarah's time truly count. This meant I had to let go of my desire for control. It also required me to be vulnerable and invite someone else into the tough moments in our home. But Sarah could handle it, and once I let her, she did an incredible job.

Suddenly I had a few hours each week to myself. What a concept! Staying at home during those hours didn't work for me, though, because if I could hear noise downstairs, I couldn't relax upstairs. I had to leave the house. The next temptation I faced came in the form of my internal drive to accomplish something: run errands, go to the grocery store, somehow earn my time away. Because I spent my days "doing" for my family, however, I needed to spend the majority of these moments just "being." I needed to head somewhere quiet—the library, Panera, or Starbucks—with a book and journal in hand. Sipping hot tea and eating something I had not cooked rejuvenated me. Now the hours we invested in a sitter truly mattered. I returned home with a little extra energy, making me a better mom when I walked through the door.

We introverted mothers typically learn about ourselves through this process of trial and error. We start out trying to do the things we see other moms doing: the large playgroups, the loud crowds, a life on the go. As we notice what drains and fuels us, we begin to understand the women God created us to be and how we operate best. We grow into ourselves, which translates into more peace for our family. We find a new level of freedom as we come into our own. And yet there's something that can trip us up, especially in our productivity-driven society. We get *self-care* confused with *self-improvement*. The first changes our lives, but the second diminishes our reserves even more.

SELF-CARE VERSUS SELF-IMPROVEMENT

Have you ever returned from a few hours "off" just as weary as when you left the house? I have and still do at times. What makes all the difference is what's going on in my head while I'm away. Since introverted mothers tend to be internal processors, we have many thoughts to sort through—especially when we finally get the alone time we crave. If I'm not careful, I will spend my valuable self-care minutes in a way that depletes my energy instead of renews it. It goes something like this: I finally have the chance to take a break. On the outside it may look like I'm relaxing, but on the inside my wheels whir and spin, trying to figure something out: *Do we need a new schedule for our days? Maybe reading a book would help with a child's current issue? Should I do a Google search to point me in the right direction?*

Fellow introverted mamas, this is *not* self-care! This is self-improvement, something our culture tells us to constantly strive for: always try to get somewhere other than where you are, to make yourself better. But remember, that's God's job. Because God's grace + our weakness = ENOUGH.

If I'm not intentional about this, I fall back into old patterns. It happened again the other day. After an especially challenging week, I found myself completely worn out. But I refused to take a real break. When I did have time alone, I pressured myself to try and solve the parenting problem we were struggling with. After several days of no progress, I realized my mistake. I wouldn't be able to find a magic cure to fix this issue. What I needed, instead, was rest so I could keep handling it. The next chance I had, I put my work away, grabbed my jacket, and took a long walk in the autumn sun. When I got back, I watched an episode of a historical British drama, then took a nap. Two hours later, I felt like myself again. The problems that had threatened to overwhelm me earlier had shrunk back to their proper size. Why had I not done this earlier?

The key to refreshing self-care, not to be confused with self-ishness or self-help, is acceptance. I have to accept my life, not try to solve it. I have to release my loved ones into God's hands, trusting he will care for them and get them where he wants them to be. I have to believe he will give me the insights I need at the right time, not by my attempts to force them to materialize, which leads to anxiety. I have to trust, and then I have to rest.

A HUGE List of True Self-Care Ideas for the Introverted Mom

If the aim of self-care is to restore rather than improve, what should that look like? The answer varies—because although we are all introverts, we are far from the same. So I've put together a massive list of meaningful ideas, taken from my own experience as well as those of other introverted moms who've shared their thoughts with me on social media. Select those that resonate with you, or just pick one to try when you have time alone.

And because we're never guaranteed that our breaks will last long, I've organized these by length of time, so you can find an option that works even if you only have a handful of minutes.

Give yourself permission to put the kids in front of a well-chosen video or in their rooms for a playtime, whatever it takes to give yourself the care you need. You'll find checkboxes by each selection so you can mark off the ones you've tried. That way, if you need fresh inspiration, just look for an empty space. And if you find an idea that really works for you, star or highlight it so you know it's a "go to" you can count on.

If you have fifteen minutes or less:

☐ Step outside and mindfully inhale a few deep breaths of fresh air.

☐ Share a six-second (or longer) hug with someone you love. Studies show that a hug of this length releases soothing, happiness-boosting oxytocin and serotonin!

☐ Read a favorite psalm aloud to yourself, paying attention to each word as you speak it. Put your own name in the verses if that helps you relate to God's promises in a more personal way. Try Psalm 23; 91; or 112.

☐ Light a scented candle and watch the flame flicker.

☐ Try to begin your day with a small moment of intention. In just two minutes, you can read a few verses of Scripture or a page from a favorite devotional.

☐ Enter the present moment without analyzing it. Imagine how different your life will be in five years' time and consider what you'll miss most from today.

☐ Wash your face or brush your teeth. Even a small, practical act of self-care can offer a restart after a busy morning or frantic afternoon.

☐ Spend a few minutes gazing at the sky. Relish your smallness, reminding yourself that if God cares for the sparrows, he will care for you and yours as well.

☐ Set a timer or download a chimes app to go off every thirty minutes or every hour. Use the bell as your reminder to bring God into whatever you're doing in that moment.

☐ Listen to a favorite song that makes you happy. I have a "happy" playlist for this purpose!

☐ Take one or two squares of dark chocolate to your room and eat them slowly.

☐ Decide to make this one day as complaint-free as possible. See how it changes your mood to speak positive words.

☐ Rub a favorite essential oil blend on your pulse points (wrist, throat, behind your ears), or put a few drops in a diffuser.

☐ Spend time with a pet you love.

☐ Text a dear friend, asking for or offering prayer.

☐ Look at your calendar over the next few months and block off a day just for self-care. Discuss it with the family and then reserve the date.

☐ Write down one cute thing each of your kids did when they were younger, a favorite memory you never want to forget.

☐ Prepare a snack and eat it one bite at a time, sitting down!

☐ Do a ten-minute brain dump. Jot down everything that's on your mind and free up much-needed mental space.

☐ Set a timer for fifteen minutes and enjoy reading an inspiring blog.

☐ Brew a cup of your favorite tea or coffee—and drink it without multitasking.

☐ Lie in a dark room with your favorite blanket and close your eyes. It's okay if you don't fall asleep; just rest!

☐ Take a long shower.

☐ Look in the mirror and pray over yourself the way you'd want someone to pray over you. Speak out the truth that God made you the right mother for your kids and affirm that he is faithfully working in your children's hearts.

☐ Choose to unplug from social media until tomorrow. Savor the extra quiet.

☐ Take a walk, even if only a lap or two around the house.

☐ If you need to mentally check out for a few minutes, set a timer and enjoy an app guilt-free on your phone.

☐ Go into your garden or yard and notice its details: touch a tree, smell a flower, feel the grass, watch an insect or bird.

☐ Write a list of every good thing, no matter how small, each of your family members has done today.

☐ Light a candle and read a poem aloud to yourself. Look for a poetry anthology to keep at your bedside. I recommend the *Poetry Teatime Companion* by Julie Bogart.

☐ Download a meditation app for a calming ritual when you need it.

☐ Write a love note from God to you or from you to God.

☐ Sit by a fireplace, staring at the flames and listening to the crackling logs.

☐ Write a list of all you've done for your family today, a tangible reminder that no one else can take your place.

☐ If you can't get away completely, go sit in your car where you can keep an eye on the house but still have a few minutes of calm.

☐ Let your mind wander without judging your thoughts or trying to control them. Just notice what you're thinking and then release it.

☐ Set a timer for fifteen minutes and watch a few funny videos online without worrying about productivity whatsoever!

☐ Say a prayer out loud, then answer yourself with what you think God might say back to you.

☐ Take a few moments to look at family photographs from five or more years ago.

☐ Help something grow: plant a seed, water the garden, or just marvel at things that blossom in the wild.

☐ Look at your to-do list and cross off the least important item *without* doing it. Ask yourself: Which of these tasks will have mattered least in ten years' time? Practice letting go—of both tasks and perfectionism.

☐ Grab your favorite children's picture book and read it to yourself!

☐ Declutter a surface or area that's been bothering you lately. After fifteen minutes, stop, even if you aren't completely done.

☐ Humble yourself and ask someone (family member, friend, or child) for help—either practical assistance or emotional support.

☐ Create a gratitude list—one full of all the things we often take for granted.

☐ Go through your essential to-dos and beside each task, write approximately how long it will take you to do it. Add fifteen minutes to your estimate, a gift of margin to yourself.

If you have thirty minutes:

☐ Read a chapter or two of your current book. (If you don't have a current title, use this time to find one. When I need soul care, I use *The Literary Medicine Cabinet* by Haley Stewart[1] to help me choose.)

☐ Make time for a favorite hobby: a musical instrument, a craft, a puzzle, whatever you enjoy!

☐ Take a quiet walk alone—without any noise, music, or podcasts.

- ☐ "Window shop" in nature. Bring home one object that inspires you.
- ☐ Get in the car and drive, even if you don't have a destination. Listen to your favorite music or just savor the silence.
- ☐ Take a thirty-minute nap and change everything. It's not long enough to fall into a deep sleep, but just right for an afternoon reset.
- ☐ Much of a mother's work becomes undone quickly. Create something that won't unravel: some handwork (like knitting or sewing), a piece of art, a poem or journal entry, a digital photo album—anything that sounds fun and stays done!
- ☐ Pay one of your children to massage your feet or rub your back.
- ☐ Take a few extra minutes to dress up in an outfit that makes you feel beautiful.
- ☐ Multi-task in a way that actually works for self-care: download an audiobook and take it along with you on a walk, in the car, or while you're cooking.
- ☐ Get out the crayons or colored pencils and enjoy a coloring page. Buy an adult coloring book so you'll have it ready.
- ☐ Hire one of your kids to complete a project that's been lingering on your own to-do list.
- ☐ Imagine what you would say to an introverted mom friend if she told you about her hard day. Now go take that advice yourself.
- ☐ Do a task on your list to a "good enough" standard and stop there. Don't allow perfectionism to get in your way.
- ☐ Write down a list of key adjectives that you want to describe your family. When you see this in black and white, you can stop chasing things that aren't your family's priorities. You can run the race God has for you and be free.

If you have an hour:

☐ Exercise in a way that feels luxurious: dancing, swimming, an exercise class, the gym, a hike—whatever you love.

☐ Binge-read your current book—such a luxury!

☐ Watch an episode or two of a favorite show. Or take the time to look for a new one you might enjoy.

☐ Take a hot bath with Epsom salts.

☐ Buy and savor your favorite flavor of ice cream.

☐ Call a close friend or family member who "gets" you and will let you share your heart without judgment.

☐ Pick or buy yourself a small bouquet of flowers and arrange them in the spot at home that will bring you the most joy.

☐ Take time for physical self-care: paint your nails, get your hair cut—something you often neglect but that feels good after it's completed.

☐ Buy yourself a small gift: a new book, a decadent pastry, a new tea to try—anything that fits your budget and makes you feel special.

☐ Stay in bed late one morning. (Or if you're a morning person, go to bed early one night.)

☐ Create a space that's just for you: a favorite chair, corner, or nook.

☐ One evening when the kids are in bed and you're alone, watch some old family videos.

☐ Try to think of God at least once each minute for an hour. Look up "The Game with Minutes" by Frank Laubach for more details and inspiration.

☐ When you're about to leave this earth, what will have mattered most to you in each area of your life? Write this down; it will help you not be swayed by external or internal whims or expectations.

If you have a few hours or more:

☐ Go to a bookstore or library, browse the shelves, and get something new for yourself.

☐ If you enjoy it, get out the crafting or decorating supplies and make progress on a project without interruptions.

☐ Sit in a cafe reading fiction or writing in a journal.

☐ Go to one of your happy places: the ocean, the woods, the mountains, any spot that speaks to your spirit.

☐ Rewatch your favorite laugh-out-loud movie.

☐ Meet up with a kindred spirit friend.

☐ Head to bed as early as you can. If you're not tired, relish the extra downtime.

☐ Go through a drive-thru and order something delicious for yourself.

☐ Get a second happiness boost by paying for the person's treat behind you as well!

☐ Set up a date night with your spouse or make plans for a date night at home.

☐ Go somewhere in your town that looks enticing—some place you've never taken time to explore.

☐ Head to a restaurant and order a beautiful meal that someone else has made! Eat it mindfully, enjoying every bite prepared for you.

☐ Buy a new fluffy blanket and keep it in a "Mom only" area.

☐ Give yourself permission to binge-watch a few episodes of a favorite show.

☐ Stay completely offline for an entire day, letting those unplugged hours refresh your heart, mind, and spirit.

☐ Take the time to cook a healthy meal for yourself.

☐ Make plans to get away alone for one night each year if possible. This doesn't have to be a lavish or expensive vacation—just a night at a nearby hotel can be incredibly renewing.

Benjamin Franklin once wrote, "When the well is dry, we know the worth of water." All introverted mothers have experienced what happens when our wells reach empty, and it isn't pretty. I hope a few of the ideas above help keep yours full to the brim and even overflowing more often.

REFLECTIONS FOR INTROVERTED MOMS

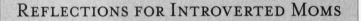

The Freedom of Discovering What's Yours

"How can you be so productive?" she asks.

I turn around to see if there's someone behind me she's speaking to.

"Me?" I answer with a nervous laugh.

"Yes, you homeschool three kids and you're a writer! How do you get so much done?"

* * *

Oh, sweet, delusional mama. I have the undone scattered across my brain.

I rarely feel as though I'm keeping all the balls in the air—a juggler who spends more time gathering on the ground than glancing toward the sky.

It's true that I have three children, I homeschool, and I write blog posts and books.

If that sounds productive, then let me pass on my secret:

I only do what's mine to do.

But that isn't as easy as it sounds, is it? When I was a new mother, I didn't know what was mine to do! I looked at all the blogs, read all the books, went to all the playgroups. I attempted to knit, make granola, and use glitter with my kids at the dining table. (Stop laughing.) And in case you're wondering, the knitting was a disaster, the granola a success, and I found glitter in cracks and crevices for months!

It takes a while to figure out who you are as an introverted mother, who you are as a person now that the lifelong job of raising children has forever altered your identity.

We find ourselves mostly through trial and error. The errors don't mean you're doing something wrong; they mean you're one step closer to knowing yourself.

Our society has made an idol of getting things done, making that our top cultural priority. But instead of wondering, "Am I checking off all the boxes?" why not ask, "Am I doing what's mine to do?"

Here's what's mine at the moment: Love my children and husband, homeschool, read, write, cook, clean (delegating those last two whenever possible now that the kids are older!).

It's a short list, but a full life. And it's enough for me. For now.

Knowing what's mine lets me focus without being pulled in all the directions all the time.

Busy mom who works all day and feels like you have nothing to show for it, don't compare your season of planting seeds with another mom's season of harvesting them.

Run your own race—this minute, this second. Be *you* unapologetically. Only do what's yours to do, and watch how you, your family, and even the world are changed because of it.

Reflections from Introverted Moms

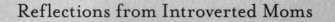

HOW DID YOUR LIFE AND YOUR FAMILY'S LIFE CHANGE FOR THE BETTER ONCE YOU UNDERSTOOD AND ACCEPTED YOURSELF AS AN INTROVERT?

My family no longer feels that an outing in a crowd is something I have to do (with them). I am enjoying my time, and they can enjoy their time, and we all feel that we had a good day. I do occasionally get into the mix, as long as I know it won't be too long or invade my personal space too much. Win / win!

LISA, UNITED KINGDOM

Life got easier and less stressful . . . I stopped putting so much pressure on myself to be what society expected and just liked being me. My family is happier because I am happier!

MARIE, AUSTRALIA

It released me from the pressure to fit in. And the more I fed my inner desire to be myself, the more I realized there is a huge part of me that's more like an extrovert.

NITIKA, MASSACHUSETTS

When I realized that making necessary phone calls, visits, or even playdates required more energy than folding ten loads of laundry or cleaning the house, I started planning accordingly. If I have to do a lot of people-y things, I plan to have some downtime later that day or the next day.

SANDRA, CANADA

There was an in-between period when I knew I was truly an introvert, and I was starting to make accommodations for that, but I would do so with guilt. I felt like I just wasn't trying hard enough, or I was giving in to my nature too much. That was rough for my family. But once I truly accepted and embraced the reality, my entire family became happier.

KIM, WASHINGTON STATE

PART 2

governing
it well

A little kingdom I possess, where thoughts and

feelings dwell;

And very hard the task I find of governing

it well.

LOUISA MAY ALCOTT,
"A LITTLE KINGDOM I POSSESS"

CHAPTER 4

no great loss

ON NAVIGATING HEARTACHE AND DISAPPOINTMENT

There's no great loss without some small gain.

LAURA INGALLS WILDER,
LITTLE HOUSE ON THE PRAIRIE

You're not going to recover from this. It's going to kill you."

Everyone remembers 2001 because of September 11's devastating tragedy, but my own world began crumbling far earlier than the Twin Towers.

The doctor's bluntness felt like a curse pronounced over my fifty-five-year-old dad and our whole family as we sat in the harshly lit, sterile room. The diagnosis? Fast-spreading pancreatic cancer. The prognosis? Three to six months. Doctor No-Bedside-Manner went on to explain the test results. A normal

CA 19–9 level in a healthy person's blood is less than 37. Dad's level? An outrageous 23,000. Even in the face of such dire news, Dad's humor lightened the mood in a way I still remember: "Well, do I at least get a trophy or something?" he asked. We laughed, then drove home and cried.

In the following months, I started making frequent trips to North Carolina from Washington DC, where Steve and I had moved as a young married couple. I wanted to spend as much time with Dad as I could. Little did we know our pain was just beginning. On April 11 I got a call at work, letting me know that my mom's dad, the tenderhearted grandfather we called Sugie, had passed away. Steve and I climbed back in the car, the six-hour drive having become a regular, loss-etched feature of our routine. Honoring and grieving Sugie's seventy-nine years of life did not come easily, though, because the heaviness of my dad's lingering disease still crushed our shoulders as though we were Atlas, burdened with the weight of the world. Too sick to attend his own father-in-law's funeral, Dad asked us to video it for him.

But before Sugie's funeral plans had even been finalized, my mom received a call from a relative on my dad's side of the family in Tennessee, where my other grandfather was also battling cancer. I sat in a plush recliner across the living room as she listened. A few moments later, she mouthed two words in my direction that caused the room to dim and sway: "He died." A new wave of shock hit me as I tried to take in this unbelievable news—both of my grandfathers dying one day apart, my father just months from death himself. In that moment it honestly felt like anyone I loved could be next, like someone was out to get us. I left the room so I wouldn't have to hear Mom tell Dad his father had died. I couldn't handle watching his shoulders sink any lower.

A typical introvert with a lot to process, I turned to my journal:

The world needs more men in it like the man my father is. Currently, I can say how my father "is," but only for another month or so, before I begin to talk about the type of man my father "was." Isn't it strange how death graduates you from one grammatical tense to another? I only wish I could spend my evenings complaining about my boss, instead of discussing Dad's condition and its fast-paced deterioration with my husband. Oh, for normal life!

Since when did "normal" consist of looking at caskets on the internet to save money, or discussing how Dad managed to keep down three bites of baked potato? But this is daily life now. Our ordinary. It isn't the evening news I am watching, thinking of those poor people who have been through so much. This is me, my life, my father . . . People are looking at our family, thinking, "Those poor people have been through so much." We are on the other side of their sympathy—how did we get here?

Not long after I wrote those words, the time came to say goodbye to my father, the only other introvert in my immediate family. His childhood had been laden with difficulties, yet God had transformed him into a man who did his best for our family. The one who had watched *Little House on the Prairie* and *Anne of Green Gables* with me countless times, who had helped me study for countless tests, who had affirmed in countless moments that I was good enough. During one of our final conversations, I sat on the edge of his hospice bed while he faded in and out of consciousness. Suddenly, I heard his voice: "I keep drifting off to sleep . . . then you move a little and it wakes me up."

I started to apologize, thinking my fidgeting had frustrated him. But he went on: "Then I open my eyes and see you sitting there, looking like a beautiful angel."

On June 12, two months after my grandfathers died, Dad passed away. After the funeral we sat in Mom's living room with the television on, a plethora of Father's Day commercials playing. I remember how hollow it felt, knowing I was now fatherless. There was no need to rush to the store for a last-minute present.

As a twenty-five-year-old, I was still figuring out who I was as an adult, a woman, and a wife. This being my first experience with grief, I tried to deal with the hurt as best I could. It pained Steve to see me upset when he couldn't fix it, and I didn't know how to talk about my feelings in a healthy and vulnerable way. We joined a small group Bible study with a few other couples that summer, and I never even mentioned to anyone that my father had just passed away. With that subconscious choice, I did what introverts tend to do—I turned my pain inward. By the time Steve and I saw smoke rising over the Pentagon and the Twin Towers collapsing on television, it felt as though the end of the world had truly come.

DEALING WITH THE TOUGH STUFF OF LIFE INTROVERT-STYLE

Pelf City—it's an okay spot to visit, but you wouldn't want to live there.

Mom has reminded me of this more times than I can count. Pelf City is code for Self Pity, our destination when life comes out of nowhere and kicks us in the teeth. It's a bad day, or week, or month, or year. We call each other and cry and allow all the feelings: It's not fair, why does he or she keep doing this, how are we going to get through it? But the rule is simple: You can make a rest stop in Pelf City, but you can't buy property and break ground on new construction. You acknowledge the hard, share it with someone you trust, then slip on your big girl pants and continue the journey.

I learned the importance of this principle the hard way as an introverted mother. For more than seven years, one of my children routinely struggled with anger. Daily rages were our reality, long past the terrible twos. I'm sure you can imagine, or perhaps know all too well yourself, how difficult it is for an introvert to recharge with screams and constant conflict in the background. Yet for the longest time, I didn't open up about what we were going through. Because my child directed most of the anger toward me, I felt like it was my problem, my fault. I kept it inside or tried to make light of it. I thought telling the truth about the tough stuff equaled "being negative" or complaining, and that in order to be a positive person and a hardworking mom, I had to ignore those feelings or at least put a spin on them. Guess what? That didn't work; it only made life harder.

A turning point came when one day, while my child was in the middle of a tantrum, I wrote to a handful of friends:

"My child has been screaming for over an hour, and I am so sad. I need you guys to know just because I don't want to feel like it's this dark secret I'm keeping, but also because I need someone to tell me that it's not all my fault. I know I can trust you and I would really value your prayers."

Typing those words was an absolute relief, and so were the kind, caring responses that arrived minutes later, letting me know I wasn't alone, offering prayers, and simply acknowledging how hard it sounded.

Truthfully verbalizing our reality is the first step in healing our hurts. Not only that, but we desperately need this kind of vulnerability in our world. After all, we don't often scroll through social media to find a photo of someone's shrieking child, do we? I get this. We use our lenses to capture beauty. But that can also lead us to think we're the only ones dealing with anything less than beautiful. When we courageously expose our personal darkness, it's impossible for it to remain shadowed and overcast. Light transforms everything, and loads are always easier to carry when distributed between two sets of shoulders.

Let's turn to the Psalms for a blueprint of how to do this. Consider Psalms 42; 56; 57; 142; 143, and many others. We can see a pattern: The writers express the reality of their current paths. They don't shy away from pain and suffering:

My enemies have set a trap for me. I am weary from distress. (Psalm 57:6 NLT)

I cry out to the LORD; I plead for the LORD'S mercy. I pour out my complaints before him and tell him all my troubles. When I am overwhelmed, you alone know the way I should turn. (Psalm 142:1–3 NLT)

Yet the writers of the Psalms don't set up camp in Pelf City, either. After a few honest verses, they turn their attention from the problem back to God's faithfulness. They recall the times he helped them in the past. And they remind themselves that God will be there this time, too:

Why am I discouraged? Why is my heart so sad? I will put my hope in God! I will praise him again—my Savior and my God! Now I am deeply discouraged, but I will remember you . . . (Psalm 42:5–6 NLT)

You keep track of all my sorrows. You have collected all my tears in your bottle. You have recorded each one in your book. My enemies will retreat when I call to you for help. This I know: God is on my side! I praise God for what he has promised; yes, I praise the LORD for what he has promised. (Psalm 56:8–10 NLT)

We can cling to this pattern when we need to deal with life's disappointments in a way that keeps us moving forward instead of in a way that keeps us feeling stuck. It's vital that we do so, because introverts who don't fully deal with heartache will find it rising to the surface repeatedly, trying to get our attention. Our bodies, minds, and spirits won't let us forget what's hidden. It may show up as chronic pain, an eating disorder, a compromised immune system, an angry outburst, or a host of other unhealthy symptoms.

To deal with periods of sadness or sorrow, Certified Life Coach and Grief Recovery Specialist Kathryn Van Auken recommends that introverts know and accept their limits, make self-care and self-compassion a top priority, and find a group (yes, an online group counts!) that allows them to share their own tough truths in an honest, safe space.[1] Loss and heartache drain any personality type, but understanding their impact on us as introverts means we can show ourselves extra kindness, setting a beautiful example for our kids—introverted or otherwise—of how to deal with hardship in their own lives.

KEEPING OUT THE SHADOWS: LESSONS
FROM L. M. MONTGOMERY

The road of literature is at first a very slow one, but I have made a good deal of progress since this time last year and I mean to work patiently on until I win—as I believe I shall, sooner or later—recognition and success.

L. M. MONTGOMERY, APRIL 9, 1897 (AGE 22)

Why yes, Maud, yes. Just a tad bit of recognition and success might be heading your way. One day a few years from now, you'll search through your idea notebook and come across a faded entry: *Elderly couple apply to orphan asylum for a boy. By mistake a girl is sent them.* She will grow in your mind, this mischievous orphan, until you can't bear to waste her on the Sunday school newspaper story you'd originally planned. Instead you'll write your first book, bringing to life a character who will go on to bring life and hope to millions. Except you won't know it yet. When the book is finished, you'll seal your heart in a large envelope and send it to four publishers, all of whom will reject your redheaded heroine. Bruised by failure, you'll pack *Anne of Green Gables* away in the bottom of an old hat box, then stumble upon her later, dust her off, decide to try one more time. And that will change everything.

I wrote it for love, not money—but very often such books are the most successful—just as everything in life that is born of true love is better than something constructed for mercenary ends.

AUGUST 16, 1907 (AGE 32)

Lucy Maud Montgomery (1874–1942; known as "Maud" to friends and family) was born on November 30, 1874, into a life marked by extreme opposites: depths of despair on one hand and highs of fame on the other. She never knew her mother, who died before Maud turned two. Her father, overcome by grief, soon left Maud in the care of her strict maternal grandparents, with whom she spent her childhood and her first years as an adult. Maud and her legendary Anne with an "e" had a lot in common: both lost parents at a young age, struggled with loneliness and felt misunderstood, had writing ambitions, lived in a world of vivid imagination, and adored their home on Prince Edward Island, Canada. Because Maud journaled prolifically, from age fourteen until her death at sixty-seven, modern-day readers have the chance to glimpse her inner world, which helps us understand her as both an introverted woman and, later, a mother.

> *It seems that Anne is a big success. One of the reviews says that "the book radiates happiness and optimism." When I think of the conditions of worry and gloom and care under which it was written I wonder at this. Thank God, I can keep the shadows of my life out of my work. I would not wish to darken any other life—I want instead to be a messenger of optimism and sunshine.*

OCTOBER 15, 1908 (AGE 33)

Perhaps I've always been drawn to Maud because it seems likely we share the same personality type—INFJ on the Myers-Briggs type indicator. One of the rarest types, the INFJ is often considered "The Advocate," someone "quiet and mystical, yet a very inspiring and tireless idealist."[2] Creative introverts who follow through with plans and ideas, we also tend to be sensitive, extremely private, and perfectionistic—qualities that lead to burnout when we're not careful.

Maud married a minister, Ewan Macdonald, at the age of thirty-six. She longed to have children, and soon after her marriage, found she was pregnant. She went on to raise two sons, Chester and Stuart. As a mother, Maud hoped to give her two boys the support she herself had lacked:

> *Oh, my darling little son, you make up for*
> *everything I have suffered and missed in life.*
> *Everything led to you—and therefore I feel that all*
> *has been for the best.*

SEPTEMBER 22, 1912 (AGE 37, AFTER HAVING HER FIRST CHILD)

But like us, Maud struggled with her adjustment to introverted motherhood. At times she expressed frustration with certain aspects of her new role. This included a lack of time to read and write, her two great passions, and the constant pressure to make progress on another book when interruptions came so regularly:

> *I often think wistfully of the quiet hours by my old*
> *window "down home," where I thought and wrote*
> *"without haste and without rest." But those days are*
> *gone and cannot return as long as wee Chester is a*
> *small make-trouble. I do not wish them back—but I*
> *would like some undisturbed hours for writing.*

MAY 21, 1913 (AGE 38)

The second half of Maud's life brought more loss her way, including the mental illness of her husband, which grew worse over time and which she fearfully attempted to conceal; the devastating loss of her second baby at birth; the early death of her dearest friend and trusted confidante; the struggle to keep developing as an author in a publishing world dominated by men; and the stress of managing her duties as a minister's wife. As the years became more challenging and her support system dwindled, Maud relied even more on her journal as a safe place to pour out her burdens. But the shadows we find in them only tell part of her story.

In a life impacted deeply by heartache, great beauty also emerged. Once, as a young mother, Maud composed a list of her favorite things: seasons, authors, trees, and so on. She included her deepest dream, to "write a book that will *live*." She didn't believe this dream could come true, yet *live* her books have. Maud made her beloved Island famous, passing its stunning treasures on to scores of readers and visitors. And that dramatic redhead of hers? She's gone on to sell over fifty million copies, placing *Anne of Green Gables* in the list of the top 25 best-selling books of all time, redeeming tragedy and making Maud the messenger of optimism she always longed to become.[3]

INTRODUCTED MOM TAKEAWAYS FROM L. M. MONTGOMERY'S LIFE

Use your journal.

Maud poured both the good and the bad into the pages of her journal. It doesn't matter if it's loose paper, a beautifully bound book, or a digital document—clearing the thoughts out of our head, particularly in difficult times, can be powerfully helpful for introverts. I like to write down my positive thoughts and gratitude to keep long-term, but after I use my digital journal for releasing negativity, I prefer to erase it. I find it beneficial to get dark thoughts out of my head, but it's not helpful for me to hold on to them forever.

But go beyond your journal, too.

When we become isolated, as Maud did during certain periods of her life, we more easily find ourselves stuck in unhealthy patterns of negative thinking, self-pity, and the false belief that we must carry all our burdens alone. But when we share openly and vulnerably with someone we trust, our problems shrink back into their proper perspective as we allow others to help and support us.

Only God determines our legacy.

The public adored Maud's work, but a few professional critics and other authors openly spoke out against it. Yet here we are, more than a hundred years later, and look whose books are still being read! Each of us has significance in God's eyes, freeing us from the need to strive, perform, or compare. When we accept what is and isn't within our control, we can focus on what matters most—obedience to his calling today.

The healing power of nature.

If you've read any of her books, you already know how much nature meant to Maud. She brought her treasured homeland to life so vividly that thousands still flock there each year, seeking out the real Lover's Lane, Haunted Wood, and the red soil of PEI.

I've seen them myself, and they are as stunning as she describes. Wherever we live, let's seek out the comfort, connection, and restoration nature provides.

God redeems pain.

Part of the reason the world continues to love Anne is because even though she has endured great hardship, she still manages to find beauty in her world. Through the novel's overwhelming success and longevity, we also see how God redeemed Maud's own brokenness, transforming it into a gift that continues to help new generations. We can trust him to do the same with the heartache and loss in our own lives.

WANT TO LEARN MORE ABOUT MAUD? CHECK OUT:

- Her most popular / well-known piece: *Anne of Green Gables* (published in 1908, when she was thirty-four)
- One of her personal favorites: *The Story Girl* (published in 1911, when she was thirty-seven)
- Something a little different: *The Blythes Are Quoted* (this manuscript turned up at her publisher's office on the day Maud died, but was never published in its entirety until 2009)
- This work about her: *Lucy Maud Montgomery: The Gift of Wings* by Mary Henley Rubio

REFLECTIONS FOR INTROVERTED MOMS

Grace for the Introverted Mom

Good morning, introverted mama.

I see you there: forehead creased, shoulders slumped, tears on cheeks.

This mothering gig isn't easy, but where did you get the idea that the whole thing is your responsibility? That their entire future depends solely on your ability to get it right?

You won't get it right and you can't do it all, but here's the thing:

You were never called to. That's why there is grace.

Grace for when the baby is on the way.

Grace for when the baby's born—when spirits are high and sleep is low.

Grace, even, for when the baby dies and your world shatters, leaving you broken, desperate, and wondering how you'll ever grasp normal again.

There's grace for when school or work routines change, and everyone scrambles to adjust. Grace, still, for when bank accounts dwindle and cupboards are bare.

There is grace for you today when your husband walks out the door on a weeklong work trip, and you know you won't have a moment of quiet for seven days.

Grace, also, for when your husband walks out the door . . . and never comes back.

In the midst of a *real* life, one of great joy and great challenge, all your offerings and sacrifices, your best efforts and your biggest try-hards—they will *never* be enough.

Good news: they aren't supposed to be.

Scripture overflows with stories of individuals who gave all they had to offer. Asked to do the impossible, they knew they weren't up for it:

a virgin birth
the parting of a sea
the multiplication of loaves and fishes

They stepped up with their imperfect sacrifice—and then: miraculously, joyfully, incredibly, what happened?

Grace filled in the gaps.

I don't know about you, but I often feel as though God has asked me to do the impossible.

When I look at these children he's entrusted to my care, when I consider all they need to be prepared for life, when I glimpse my failures again and again—well, I'm just about ready to hand in my resignation.

But it was never about what I can do or what you can do. We *cannot* do this effectively on our own. We will try our best and work our hardest and come up short every time. We will never measure up.

Hallelujah—this is a good thing! Here's what this freeing realization means:

We don't have to stress so much. An unseen partner, the best parent in the world, wants to help us raise our kids. His record is solid, and he specializes in the impossible.

So dry those eyes, introverted mom. Release that control and exhale those heavy-burdened fears.

For you, for your family, there is grace.

And for today—in this hour, this one precious, never-to-return moment—that is enough.

Reflections from Introverted Moms

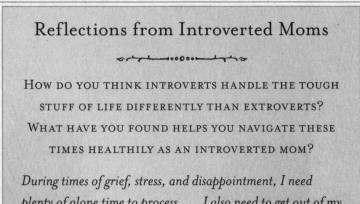

HOW DO YOU THINK INTROVERTS HANDLE THE TOUGH STUFF OF LIFE DIFFERENTLY THAN EXTROVERTS? WHAT HAVE YOU FOUND HELPS YOU NAVIGATE THESE TIMES HEALTHILY AS AN INTROVERTED MOM?

During times of grief, stress, and disappointment, I need plenty of alone time to process . . . I also need to get out of my head, so proven novels, movies (nothing new), and strenuous physical activity all work well. These times also lead me to upturn the house and my life to try and find order amongst my chaos.

JEN, AUSTRALIA

I try to share my (minor) "troubles" only once. For example, if I'm having trouble with the kids and I unload to another mom, then I don't repeat my worries again to my sister, my mother, or other friends. If I still feel the need to share, I pray about it.

JESSICA, MAINE

I keep a private journal on my computer. I also have two friends whom I message about life and struggles.

ERICA, PAPUA NEW GUINEA

Since I internally process everything, I will think things to death. I have found that high–intensity exercise helps me to not think for a bit (because I have to focus all my attention on what I'm doing) and then I can return to what I'm processing with a clearer head. It helps me to release some of the big feelings I keep chewing on and then return to the issue with the ability to more rationally process.

CASSIE, OHIO

I usually wake up earlier than normal and spend time prayer journaling, reading the Bible for comfort, and reading devotions written by women who know the pain of loss, grieving, or heartache. Even when I'm not struggling, I try to take a "Barbara Day" once a month by myself. I often process things so much between myself and God that I fail to tell my husband what I am struggling with. After twenty years of marriage, he now asks how I'm doing more, and I actually make myself open up more.

BARBARA, IRELAND

CHAPTER 5

tenderness
of heart

❧

ON MARRIAGE AND
RAISING CHILDREN

*Warmth and tenderness of heart, with an
affectionate, open manner, will beat all the
clearness of head in the world . . .*

JANE AUSTEN, *EMMA*

You like books more than me."

Aren't the first years of marriage fun / hard / confusing?
This goes for any couple, no matter his and her personality types.
Add in a complication, like an introvert marrying an extrovert,
and hold the line for extra drama, quiet style. While we're at it,
why not move in with twelve teenagers for a few more kicks?

It happened like this: The year after the tragedies I mentioned in the previous chapter, Steve and I had an opportunity come our way. Still living in Washington DC, where rent bills ran high and our student loans even higher, we were offered the chance to partner with a local nonprofit organization. In exchange for serving as "house parents" to twelve recent high school graduates and college students selected as interns, we could live rent-free. We had to make dinner for them once a week, shop for basic staples like bread and milk, and keep the house from burning down. Of course, this was on top of our full-time jobs: Steve's as an operations manager for a television / video company and mine as an aide to children with special needs in a nearby school. Translation: I spent all day with little people, then drove home to spend all evening with larger people. (Introverted translation: Too. Many. People!)

We knew then and can see even more clearly now that this opportunity arrived as an answer to prayer. We'd had it on our hearts for some time to pay off our debts, but as newlyweds living in an expensive city, that was easier said than done. After just one year in the intern house, however, we eliminated our student loans as well as a small credit card bill and our car loan, a feat that could have taken us a decade otherwise. This enabled us to answer God's call later that year to begin a new life as volunteers with Mercy Ships, and to reach our goal of being debt-free before we started a family.

Yet God's blessings often come with character-building challenges. We'd only been married a few years at this point, so living with a dozen young adults stretched our relationship. Like the time four teens decided that midnight would be the perfect opportunity to break out the Monopoly board at the table right outside our bedroom door. The evenings we'd return after full days of work and need to prep dinner for fifteen people. The times when we had to motivate young adults away from home for the first time to clean their shockingly dirty rooms. Some days I'd get home before Steve and have an hour to read or think. Then, when he arrived, I'd be ready to hang out. But if we happened to get home from work at the same time, introverted Jamie longed for a little quiet, something extroverted Steve didn't always need.

Once that year, I snapped a photo of Steve reading a mystery in our overstuffed pastel blue-and-pink plaid (Yes, plaid!) armchair. After I had the photo printed, I laminated it and turned it into a bookmark, one I still have. On the back, Steve had written: "I love you more than books." So sweet! And maybe written with a teensy question mark, to see if I would say the same about him. Let me set the record straight here: I have never loved books more than my husband, yet I need my books so I can love my husband even more.

Sparkle and Glow: On Differing Personality Types in Marriage

Extroverts sparkle, introverts glow. Extroverts are fireworks, introverts are a fire in the hearth.

Sophia Dembling, Introverts in Love

We argued the other night. Somehow what began as a discussion developed a heated tone. I saw the change come over his face and tried to back my way out. My nervous system began its fight or flight response: abort, abort! But I didn't know how to fix it.

What he said made no sense to me, and obviously the feeling was mutual. I wanted him to tell me I was doing a good job; he wanted to verbally process. As an always-and-forever internal processor, I didn't recognize the signals.

After emotions died down, Steve explained that verbal processing doesn't mean he's set his opinions in stone; he just needs a listening ear. I made him feel small by not hearing him out. And when he eventually understood that I only wanted to feel affirmed and approved, I saw his look of shock. He thought I wanted to talk it out! By pushing through the discomfort instead of skirting around it, we reached an understanding that helped us move forward. And this is after twenty years of marriage. Clearly, we still have much to learn.

Has anything like this happened to you, too? It reminds me of practicing basic foreign language skills with someone in another country. You manage to combine a few words and phrases with some darn good hand gestures. Sometimes you triumph and get your message across, feeling like a pro. Other times you smile, giggle nervously, pretend to understand, then accidentally walk into the men's room. At times we do speak two languages in marriage, especially when our partner's personality differs from ours. But with a little clarity and understanding, extroverts and introverts can appreciate and build on each other's strengths.

He loves you; you love him. What could be the problem? Uh, this chapter isn't long enough to list them all! Couples starting out face a host of issues: jobs, money, whether and when to have children, extended family dynamics, and more. These topics came up in our premarital counseling, but if we had also taken a personality test and received a practical explanation of the results, I believe it would have made for an easier transition into life together. This would be just as helpful if couples share introversion or extroversion, or like us, have a blend of both.

For a long time in our marriage, I felt like Steve didn't always get me. I knew we were both doing our imperfect best to love, respect, and honor each other. But when we had inevitable disagreements or misunderstandings, it seemed as though we had failed to live up to the marriage ideal in my head. Only years later did I understand that we would always have differing viewpoints as different people. Expecting Steve to be everything to me was unfair, setting him up for failure before he'd even begun.

Instead of looking to Steve for help with every issue, I now turn to a few close friends when I need to discuss something with a fellow introvert. This kind of support is especially vital for single introverted moms, who carry extra burdens and shoulder parenting challenges alone. Patty McMullen from Illinois told me she views her role as a single mom "more like plate spinning than juggling. I keep tapping each plate just enough to keep each one from falling. Some days are better than others. Sometimes the plates develop a serious wobble; some days I have everything spinning smoothly."

My friend Shawna Wingert, writer of the blog Not the Former Things, who spent five years as a single mother, described the intense responsibility like this: "Every single day, it was all on me—providing, nurturing, caring for, teaching, disciplining—it felt like there was no safe place to just be."[1] If she could go back, Shawna says she would remind herself that it's okay to ask for and accept help. She sees now that there were people in her life who wanted to support her, but at times her introversion, as well as the embarrassment she felt over her situation, kept her from taking them up on their offers. And some of the advice Karyn Ashley-Smith of Connecticut would offer fellow single mothers is to "not worry about what your friends will think of your house if you invite them over. Real friends won't notice . . . true friends will already know that it is what it is."

Single or married, we need to lean on our friends. When I talk with or send a desperate text to Carrie or Jill or Kara or Kelly, it's comforting to hear them respond, "Yep, I totally know what you mean" or "I struggle with that, too." It's been freeing to give my spouse a break from having to fully understand me. We don't always have to get each other in order to love each other well and build a strong life together.

HUSBANDS, IF YOUR WIFE IS AN INTROVERT, HERE'S WHAT YOU NEED TO KNOW:

Even though your husband doesn't need to grasp every detail of your introverted intricacies, he still might appreciate an overview of how his wife ticks. That's why I wrote the following section. Feel free to pass the book over, read it aloud, leave it out for him, or read it yourself and summarize in conversation later.[2]

Being an introvert isn't better, or worse, than being an extrovert.

Recent studies suggest that between one-third to one-half of the entire US population, male *and* female, are introverts. Western society often champions extroverts as winning individualists, but in other cultures the reverse is viewed as ideal. We all have strengths to offer as well as weaknesses to overcome, no matter the specifics of our personality.

*Contrary to stereotypes, introverts enjoy people
time, especially with those they are close to
(like you, your children, and good friends).*

But people time, even with close relationships, eventually drains
an introvert. They typically recharge best alone.

*This means one of the kindest things you
can do for the woman you love is to make
sure she has some quiet each day.*

Encourage her to do this, guilt-free, even if it means giving the
kids a little screen time to make it happen.

*Your introverted wife does not love books or
(insert her hobby here) more than you!*

But expecting her to be there for an in-depth conversation right
at the end of a busy day might not be realistic. Even extroverts
like to have downtime after a hectic weekday, and for introverted
moms, this is absolutely essential to healthy bodies, minds, and
spirits. Understand that if you give her thirty minutes to an hour
to take a break, you'll reap the rewards.

*Use these insights to help plan and
spend your social energies.*

Going out to dinner as a couple or with close friends? Totally!
Asking her to join you at a crowded business event where she
knows no one and you'll be working most of the time? Maybe give
her a pass. Of course, this is marriage, and you will both make
sacrifices for each other, but working within natural tendencies
when possible will enable both of you to avoid burnout.

You hit the jackpot.

Healthy introverts have the capacity to be rock stars when it comes to relationships because they naturally prefer the deep over the shallow and quality over quantity. By helping her thrive, you help everyone within your home thrive as well, including yourself.

LOUD AND PROUD: ON RAISING EXTROVERTED CHILDREN AS AN INTROVERTED MOM

Introvert and Extrovert sittin' in a tree
K-I-S-S-I-N-G
First comes love, then comes marriage
Then comes an extrovert in a baby carriage!

I had my earliest clue when he was only nine months old. We'd taken our first family trip to England, Steve's home, since having a baby. Little Jonathan proved to be quite the world traveler, taking after Mom and Dad when it came to being jolted from place to place with ease. Once at our destination, he met a host of aunts and uncles (Steve is the oldest of six) and loved his position as the center of attention. One hot summer evening, we returned from an outing, Jonathan past his regular bedtime and clearly tired. I took him to the loft bedroom and tucked him in, opening the windows so the heat wouldn't be stifling. Then I joined the family in the back garden to eat dinner and enjoy the sun.

Immediately, the crying began. Usually a sleeper you could count on, my babe just wouldn't settle down. Maybe it was the temperature, maybe it was the fun he could hear through the open window. I didn't even know for sure yet whether I was a cry-it-out mom or a pick-him-up mom, and I worried what others would think of me no matter which decision I made. But finally, I could take it no longer. I marched back up two flights of stairs, rescued my weepy little man, and brought him down again. And when he saw everyone in the backyard? My red-faced tyke burst into a wide smile, raised his hand, and started waving. An extrovert in a baby carriage, indeed.

Later God added another extrovert (as well as one introvert) to our family. Over the years, a few guideposts have helped me swim through the unfamiliar waters of raising an extrovert without drowning. I share them with you in the hopes that they might offer you a needed lifeline as well:

Let them talk. You can listen.

My extroverted children tend to talk. To me, to their brother and sister, to themselves, to anyone visiting. And when they were younger? To the garbage truck worker, the recycling man, the mail carrier, the UPS lady, and any neighbor passing by. They need to know how to stay quiet, of course, but they also need to discuss their many ideas. So I try to let them. Yes, this can be draining, but it can also work well, since introverted moms tend to be good listeners who don't always want to chitchat ourselves.

Compromise is key.

Help your young extroverts get the social stimulation they need, but in a way that works for both of you! Don't immediately sign up to chauffeur kids to playdates, classes, and clubs, assuming you must sacrifice your own needs to meet theirs. Think it through before making promises and creating expectations.

Look for win-wins.

When choosing activities, look for those that will fit you as an introvert, too. Playing with neighbors in the backyard while you sip tea in the house? A win-win. A visit to the home of a close friend and her children? A win-win. Weekly classes or clubs where you drop off your extroverts and hang out at a coffee shop for an hour? Definitely a win-win.

Friends matter, but family counts, too.

Extroverts recharge through time spent with others, so they *need* time with others. My extroverts love new experiences and meeting people, and as they get older this matters more. But I consider it an extra bonus that my kids hang out with their siblings often, too. I hope these relationships flourish for a lifetime, so I want to cultivate them as best I can now.

Meet your own needs and teach your kids to do the same.

If our kids think we're responsible for meeting their personality-related needs, we're teaching the wrong lesson. If we fly into action each time someone utters, "Mom, I'm bored," our children learn to turn to something (or someone) outside of themselves to get what they need, building a habit that may backfire later on. Instead, let's model appreciation for our differences, letting our extroverts stretch us out of our comfort zones while we also teach them that time alone is important for everyone. As introverted moms, we either fuel ourselves or drain ourselves with the choices we make, and so can our children.

Alone, Together: On Connecting With and Raising Introverts

Don't just accept your child for who she is; treasure her for who she is . . . Introverted children are often kind, thoughtful, focused, and very interesting company, as long as they're in settings that work for them.

Susan Cain, *Quiet*

On the surface, we don't seem to have much in common. He was born in Liberia, West Africa; I was born in North Carolina, USA. Yet God gave us a huge gift: he made us both introverts, then used adoption to cross oceans and put us in the same family. The older Elijah gets, the more grateful I feel for this personality trait we share, which keeps us from being completely outnumbered by the energetic extroverts we live with.

How can you tell if you're raising introverts? Well, you might recognize yourself in them: a tendency to concentrate deeply, a preference for small groups, a personality that would rather observe before plunging into the action. As introverted kids grow, they'll naturally crave and likely seek out alone time. And when they don't get it? Trouble follows.

However, don't expect that an introverted child will necessarily be a quiet one. My Elijah has, at different times in his life, been the loudest person in our house, banging on makeshift drums, defeating imaginary enemies in his room, shrieking outside like a wild animal. As long as he controls the noise, he's fine. But when he was a youngster and I took him somewhere loud, his hands immediately went over his ears, blocking out the extra stimulation. The types of outings he enjoyed gave me clues until it became clear that I had a kindred spirit under my roof. If you have introverts as well, here are a few ways you can set them up for success, at home and in the world:

Protect your introvert's refueling time.

This means making afternoon quiet a priority, complete with books or audiobooks, even after your child has given up napping. If your older introvert attends school all day, this downtime will be vital. You'll want to rethink the scheduling of extracurriculars and get creative about how to give your child a break before requirements like homework or chores.

Help your introvert role-play, but also let him be himself.

When headed out socially, take time to practice conversations that might arise and give your child a chance to think through their responses. Bear in mind, however, that your little one is unlikely to start jabbering with strangers. That's okay, too. You've probably noticed the world lacks good listeners; we could use more of them!

Find special ways to let her shine.

As our introverts get older, it's important to find a space that allows them to stand out without being overshadowed by their extroverted siblings. This both reminds our introverts that they have something unique to offer the world and helps us follow Susan Cain's advice that "the secret to life is to put yourself in the right lighting. For some, it's a Broadway spotlight; for others, a lamplit desk."[3] The right lighting changes everything!

Help him understand himself.

Using empowering, positive words, I've had several conversations with Elijah over the years about what it means to be an introvert. We talk about our strengths, like our sensitivity and the thoughtful insights we bring to others. We talk about enjoying people, yet also needing to be by ourselves. We also talk about confidently being who God made us to be, while learning when and how to step out of our comfort zones.

Offer what you once needed.

One of my favorite parts of raising an introvert is being able to celebrate him. In some respects, it's a do-over—a chance to provide the insight, understanding, and boosts of self-assurance I didn't always receive growing up in an extrovert-dominant society. It's also a chance to keep an eye out for unhealthy warning signs of burnout and to take action by safeguarding his alone time. I've found this to be a healing process for myself, too.

REFLECTIONS FOR INTROVERTED MOMS

All Different Kinds of Beautiful

We share four walls, yet live in a world of difference.
You: outspoken and bold; Me: heart-soft and mild.
Amazed by the other: "Do we even speak the same
    language?"
love stretching our borders all the while.

Now we've grown our ranks, and what feels foreign
    multiplies.
Some can't stop chattering. Some sensitive, tender.
I shake my head in awe: "Do we even speak the same
    language?"
love stretching my borders all the while.

We make our way in the world, together.
We don't look alike, talk alike, think alike, act alike.
Yet somehow belong to each other,
every one of us a different kind of beautiful.

Our contrasts have not always been valued
Told we were "too much" or "not enough"
in trouble for fitting in, in trouble for standing out,
before us the hard work of unconditional love.

Now's our chance to rewrite childhood scripts,
To proclaim splendor in place of shame.
Expose old hurts and wash them clean,
to speak truth over a new generation:

Tell them that whether they're quiet or loud,
whether they prefer one friend or a crowd,
God put all different kinds of beautiful in this world.
A whole host of ways to express and show love:

Love can keep silent or speak up.
Love can heal hurts or just hold them.
Love can look at weak places and see strength,
look at strong places and see the cracks.

Tell them that her laugh and his tears,
that his focus and her concerns,
that your intensity, and my empathy,
each reflect the multifaceted One who made us all.

So get out your guidebooks and dictionaries,
let's learn to speak each other's languages.
Attempt to understand even what makes no sense,
knowing that love always leads to better translations.

People don't go traveling for more of the same,
they look for uniqueness, sights yet unseen.
Get out their cameras to capture, share it.
And what once seemed foreign one day feels like home.

May we aim for that within these four walls:
worlds valued, even when not understood.
Seeking to not just guard and defend opinions,
but to let guards down, learn from one another:

Each of us, a different kind of beautiful.
Each of us, a treasure unmatched in any land.

Reflections from Introverted Moms

DO YOU HAVE MORE INTROVERTS OR MORE
EXTROVERTS IN YOUR FAMILY? HOW DO YOU TRY TO
BALANCE EACH TYPE'S NEEDS, INCLUDING YOUR OWN?

*We're definitely a split house. My three-year-old son and I
are introverts, and my nine-year-old daughter and husband
are extroverts. I try to send my husband and daughter out
together, which works well. My son and I like to hang out or
watch Dad and Sister do things. The hardest part, so far, is
explaining to my daughter that her baby brother is perfectly
happy watching her do something instead of doing it with her.*

DINAH, COLORADO

*My eldest daughter is an extrovert. I am not. She will talk
with the cashier in the supermarket, and will even explain
to my doctor how I've been. She's seven years old. What I've
done to let her cultivate her personality is enroll her in ballet
class. That way she is learning discipline, respect, and being
quiet when needed, but she also gets to spend time running,
jumping, and talking with her friends.*

SARAI, PUERTO RICO

*I am an introvert, but my hubby is an extreme introvert and
a highly sensitive person. We balance this by making sure he
has a night or two a week when I don't expect him to socialize
with me after the kids go to bed. (He may sit with me while he*

reads or games, but we don't talk or do the same activity.) He also supports my nights out to do ministry work or socialize when I can't stand being at home anymore and need adult company.

BETHANY, PENNSYLVANIA

We're five in our family and three of our members are extroverts. The key is to acknowledge and respect each other's personalities, especially for the two of us who are introverts— to really take time to be by ourselves, to recharge, even just for a couple of minutes, several times a day.

MAIA, PHILIPPINES

Our whole family seems to be introverted, just varying to the degree. My husband is more social than I am, and our two young girls seem to be more like him. They like being social, but also really appreciate having private "quiet time" in their room. We all disappear into various spaces throughout the day as needed, but still come together as a family frequently (where we often sit in comfortable silence). I grew up in a family of all introverts and my own little family resembles that dynamic.

TIFFANY, WISCONSIN

CHAPTER 6

pruned down and branched out

ON STRETCHING OUT OF
OUR COMFORT ZONES

*I'm not a bit changed—not really. I'm only just
pruned down and branched out. The real me—back
here—is just the same.*

L. M. MONTGOMERY, *ANNE OF GREEN GABLES*

Y ou're not exactly the way I imagined you based on your
interview."

Hmmm, really? I wonder why? Could it be because the night
before said interview, I propped myself up in bed until late, flip-
ping through the classic *How to Win Friends and Influence People* by
Dale Carnegie? A coveted job had become available, one that

tons of college students like myself would be going after, a cushy position that let you work on campus in one of the department offices. I wanted this opportunity, but I knew competition would be stiff. I only had one shot to make a first impression, and I couldn't hold back—there wasn't time for them to get to know introverted Jamie.

So I went into that interview and extroverted my butt off. I followed Dale Carnegie's bullet points to the letter: I made eye contact, smiled and laughed, chitchatted and asked interesting questions, listened intently, and voila: I got the job! A few months later, one of my new bosses said the words above, noting that "real-life Jamie" seemed a little different than "interview Jamie," but by that point I had proven myself capable of doing the work.

Some people might think this sounds inauthentic, but I disagree. In the job interview I was still myself, simply using learned and practiced skills to showcase my qualities. The way I acted was the way I might act with Steve, a close friend, or my family. In this instance, I needed to behave that way with strangers, too, so they could get a glimpse of my strengths. And afterward? You better believe I went home to nap and watch mindless television. That extroverting took all my mojo.

When we understand ourselves as introverted women, we can respect and value how God made us, *and* we can push beyond our natural boundaries when he calls. We don't want to use our personality as an excuse to avoid hard things or as a license for selfishness. We want to honor ourselves, but we don't want to limit ourselves. Figuring this out is an art, not a science, requiring a flow that we get better at through taking chances and making mistakes.

Adopting two children internationally, moving overseas when Steve and I first married, choosing to homeschool my kids, putting my writing out there for the world to criticize—there have been many times when God has stretched me beyond my typical levels of comfort. It's only through his strength that I've done any of it, yet it hasn't always been as hard as it sounds. What I've found is that when God wants me to do something, he works in my heart until I *want* to do it, or at least until I fully know it's the right thing to do. As Hannah Whitall Smith wrote in her beautiful book, *The Christian's Secret of a Happy Life*, "Having surrendered (your) will into the keeping of the Lord, he works in it to will and to do of His good pleasure, and the soul finds itself really wanting to do the things God wants it to do. It is always very pleasant to do the things we want to do, let them be ever so difficult of accomplishment, or involve ever so much of bodily weariness."[1] Bodily weariness? This makes me wonder if Hannah herself was a fellow introverted mother.

God doesn't drag us off, kicking and screaming, to do that which we despise and which goes against the very natures he gave us. Instead he changes our desires as we seek him, then equips us to fulfill his leading, even when it might be difficult. Understanding our introversion, therefore, doesn't mean we attempt to avoid challenges, but that we recognize challenges ahead of time and come up with a plan for how to handle them. I think most introverted moms know this quite well, but not everyone does.

"So how do you make yourself *do* stuff? Does your husband prompt and encourage you to get out there?" asked an extroverted friend. Steve and I joked about this later, since I tend to be the one in our marriage who catches a vision for something new, then tries to pray / convince him to jump on the bandwagon with me. We introverted moms stretch ourselves every day, because normal life as mothers pushes us outside our comfort zones regularly! And all that stretching gives us a fine-tuned self-awareness of the times when we need to move beyond what comes naturally, for our own good or someone else's.

EVEN IF IT'S NOT A DEFINITE YES, IT COULD STILL BE A DEFINITE YES

Have you heard of the book *Essentialism: The Disciplined Pursuit of Less* by Greg McKeown? Several friends of mine raved about it, so I bought a copy. My biggest takeaway? To only say "yes" to the activities in life I know emphatically that I'm called to and / or absolutely *love* (within reason—hello laundry and dishes and meal prep).

By saying "no" to everything else, we free up the energy that often gets spent on just "okay or good" activities. The author calls this the power of extreme criteria: "If the answer isn't a definite yes, then it should be a no."[2] Finally, a guidepost I could work with to simplify decision making! I started saying "no" left, right, and center. For years I had bowed to internal or external pressure to do certain things, and now I felt the freedom to take into account my own personality, without guilt, when accepting or declining opportunities. Remarkably, I also found the author's claim true: by narrowing down my yeses, I had more energy to give to them, which in turn made them more successful and effective.

Then came Steve's fortieth birthday. His mum flew in from the UK so we could head to Turks and Caicos for five whole days alone, a record time away from the kids. We rented a sweet island apartment and couldn't wait to soak up the sun (especially because of the New England snow we'd left behind). My idea of a relaxing beach vacation included reading, hanging out, and going to an occasional restaurant. Perfection! But to my extroverted husband, this didn't equal enough excitement. He wanted to drive around the island, explore, hunt for the *very* best beaches, and—are you ready for this?—join one of those boats full of tourists to go snorkeling. When I heard this, my introverted brain began firing off warnings in rapid succession: "Red alert, red alert! Not a definite yes, not a definite yes!" You mean we're taking several hours out of our limited vacation time to surround ourselves with total strangers? Add in jumping off the boat in front of everyone to snorkel (cue flashbacks of watching Jaws as a young child). Oh, and did I mention that my last time on a small boat, I nearly threw up?

Still in the aftermath of digesting *Essentialism*, I was heady with my newfound decision making freedom. It took me about two seconds to realize, beyond a shadow of any doubt, that this snorkeling expedition was not a definite yes for me. Not only that, Steve understood and said he was more than happy to go without me. So I dropped him off and drove back to our rental for a few peaceful hours of quiet. Looking back, although I'm proud of myself for saying no, I'm not sure I made the right choice.

To explain, let me borrow a few words from Gretchen Rubin's *The Happiness Project*: "Happiness doesn't always make you feel happy."[3] I believe this wisdom holds especially true for introverts. What brings joy long-term doesn't necessarily bring it in the moment. You can think of examples, I'm sure. Exercising comes straight to my mind. Its boost of endorphins has been scientifically proven to improve our moods, yet I don't always thrill at the thought of taking a walk or putting on an exercise video. Happiness researchers have even found that the act of "extroverting" correlates with increased happiness.[4] This doesn't mean that extroverts are necessarily happier than introverts, but that putting ourselves out there in relationships leads to joy. For introverts, the majority of our extroverting will take place within small groups of close friends and family. But not always.

Back in 2013 our family had the chance to spend six weeks in the Philippines, traveling for my husband's work as CEO of the anti-human-trafficking organization Love146. When this opportunity arrived, I was both eager and terrified. Talk about a stretch! All the travel, logistics, overwhelming details, not knowing how the kids would respond—though exciting, on the surface it wasn't an immediate yes. But I'd recently finished the book *10—10—10* by Suzy Welch, and it helped me leap into the trip, introverted feet first. She suggests that when any decision comes your way, you don't solely consider how you feel about it right now, but also how you'll feel about it in one year and in ten years. That made it a cinch to decide. I knew there would be overstimulation and moments of feeling drained, but I also knew that I would have forgotten most of them in ten years' time. What would remain? The memories of an extraordinary family adventure created while helping children in the Philippines. It hasn't even been ten years since that trip, but this is already true.

Consider the early years of raising young children. Have you ever revisited photos or videos of a tough parenting season, and now you laugh at the kids' cuteness or even their mischief? What a gift! Those moments were difficult to live through, yet now you're glad you did. (And you might be glad they're over; that's okay, too.) I occasionally wish that I could feel constant joy *in* those hard moments as well, but sometimes joy comes with the sunrise—and sometimes with the sunset. Does it really matter, though, when both are stunning and worth savoring?

Back to Turks and Caicos. I'll never know for sure, but I can't help wondering if that snorkeling trip could have been one of those "delight in hindsight" moments. Reflecting on the experience afterward led me to revise my essentialism guidepost: "If it's not a definite yes *for anyone in my family*, it's a definite no." This still weeds out loads of opportunities not worth our attention, but with kids in the house, we're guaranteed plenty of worthy yeses to tug us out of our comfort. Of course, we don't have to be martyrs, following the family's every whim. We just need to take brave steps when and where God leads. Let's dare to say yes and wait for the joy, even if we wait a while. It will come.

A (HUSHED) SHOUT-OUT TO THE HIGHLY SENSITIVE

Needing one (or sometimes two) days to recover after a crowded, loud event. Having sore muscles at the end of a hard day. Empathizing with a sad news headline so keenly that I struggled to function. Lacking the energy some of my friends seemed to have. And feeling less than, thanks to all of the above. These have been constants for most of my life, yet I didn't understand them, even in light of my introversion, until a few words I stumbled upon online left me wide-eyed amazed.

I can't remember how it happened, but several years ago another blogger pointed me to the website of Dr. Elaine Aron, a psychologist who had identified a new personality trait she called "high sensitivity." According to Dr. Aron, "highly sensitive people have an uncommonly sensitive nervous system. It means you are aware of subtleties in your surroundings. It also means you are more easily overwhelmed when you have been out in a highly stimulating environment for too long, bombarded by sights and sounds until you are exhausted." What? Me, me, me! I also discovered that I share this trait with 15–20 percent of the entire population, that it appears more often in introverts but can appear in extroverts, and that biologists have even recognized it in over a hundred species.[5]

If, like me, you're both an introverted *and* a highly sensitive mama, doesn't the awareness bring a deep "aha" to your soul? Finally, so much makes sense. How that experience you'd looked forward to ended up draining you. How you don't always enjoy events or activities the way you imagined you would. How sometimes you sense your brain moving and processing differently than the norm. And how you pick up, without even trying, facial expressions and body language in a room, feeling like you need to carry the emotions of others and prevent conflict.

Recently Steve and I sat down to plan the itinerary for an upcoming family trip to England, Scotland, and Ireland. As we looked at the calendar and schedule, I felt a familiar sense of overwhelm threatening to grow. Each day contained so much "fun" potential (and I am beyond grateful for the chance to travel), yet my mind could also foresee the impact of jet lag, the reality of overstimulation, and the challenge of staying in a variety of locations and cities.

Remembering the lesson gleaned from our Caribbean trip, however, I said an enthusiastic "yes!" to the outings most important to us—knowing I'll look back on them fondly—and dared to plan with courage, not anxiety. As we talked more, though, we recognized that at times it might not be wise for me to join in every single activity. We'd say things like, "Maybe you could take the kids into the city while I stay behind for quiet," or "Since we'll be recovering from jet lag here, let's give ourselves an extra day before heading to York." Later Steve remarked, "Years ago, planning like this would have frustrated me. I would have thought you were just being dramatic. But now I understand that this is a legitimate need you have on a physical, emotional, and mental level. That's one of the benefits of learning about personality—being able to know each other in a deeper way, then using that knowledge to love one another better."

Another of Dr. Aron's stories helped me accept my love / hate relationship with travel. In her well-known book, *The Highly Sensitive Person*, she describes a trip she took to England before fully understanding her own sensitivity. There to promote a novel she'd written, the journey represented the fulfillment of a dream she'd had for years. "Of course, I got sick and hardly enjoyed a minute of the trip," she writes. But when viewed through the lens of her high sensitivity, she later realized that the entire experience had simply been too exciting. And while this goes for travel, it also goes for any out-of-the-ordinary event as an HSP. In Dr. Aron's words, "HSPs just don't do change well, even good changes."[6]

So what exactly is a highly sensitive mama to do? Anne Bogel, blogger at *Modern Mrs. Darcy* and author of the personality book *Reading People*, wrote a post on my blog years ago titled, "Self-Care for the Highly Sensitive Parent." She states that whereas "interacting with people drains introverts; sensory input—sights, smells, sounds, emotional stimulation—drains highly sensitive people." Her suggestions include trying to begin your morning calmly, embracing routine to cut down on decision making, building quiet into your daily rhythm, controlling clutter to lessen visual overwhelm, and saving extra stimulation like social media until after your workday ends.[7] These tips gave me a much-needed life-line to cling to when I first became aware of this trait in my life.

One last caution, though, which I hope this whole chapter makes clear: *You are so much more than your personality.* Introversion, high sensitivity, or any other attribute you identify with isn't some box in which to trap yourself, with a label slapped to the side reading, "Beware: Introvert" or "Fragile: Highly Sensitive Contents." These terms do not define us or give us identity. These words are merely tools. Through understanding them, we become more fully alive and more fully ourselves than ever before, knowing when to step out and when to retreat, when to open up and when to turn inward. Think of Bilbo Baggins in *The Hobbit*, desperate to maintain his comfort when Gandalf shows up at the door, yet finally throwing caution aside, shouting, "I'm going on an adventure!"[8] I want to be a Bilbo, ready to fling wide the door and leap whenever God knocks.

REFLECTIONS FOR INTROVERTED MOMS

Kneeling in the Dirt, Waiting for the Growth

"I am the true vine, and my Father is the gardener. He cuts off every branch in me that bears no fruit, while every branch that does bear fruit he prunes so that it will be even more fruitful."

JOHN 15:1–2

In certain seasons, the land lies fallow. Nothing comes up; nothing goes down. Sometimes I love this. The rest. The silence. Sometimes, desperate to produce, I hate it. But my plot is not my own; it belongs to the gardener. He has a unique timetable, a faithful track record. Eventually, one day a tiller arrives, stirs things up. I am unearthed, exposed, inside out.

Clinging to comfort, I grasp for security. Yet Jesus calls, "Come, plant with me. Live a messy and glorious adventure, dirt under your nails." He pats the soil, invites me to kneel, shows me seeds of all shapes and sizes. How can I be responsible for my crop when I don't even know what's going in the ground?

With a tendency to make everything about me, I want to know how it will turn out. I long for guaranteed results and a full harvest. But he says nothing about outcomes, only that he'll stay. Remain. We crouch side by side, on days when the sun warms us and days when rains threaten to wash us away.

Finally I glimpse the first strand of life, pushing through dark earth. At the right time another joins it. And another. Then a whole field of green! I celebrate—until I see weeds thriving, too. It isn't my job to prune, though. Only to stay planted. I watch as he goes lower, pulling out what doesn't belong, what threatens to steal growth.

When the harvest arrives, I'm shocked. Vivid colors, abundant life everywhere! A yield so bountiful it nourishes my self, my family, and others as well. He has planted the perfect crop that suited my soil, and every once in a while, a surprise. Only a loving, master gardener could see beyond the mess of dirt, the potential below the surface.

As I turn to express my thanks, I glimpse him up ahead. He's extending another invitation. And this time? I see my children by his side: *"Come, plant with me . . ."*

Reflections from Introverted Moms

WHEN DO YOU FIND IT NECESSARY AND BENEFICIAL
TO NUDGE YOURSELF TO "EXTROVERT" MORE AS AN
INTROVERTED MOM? WHAT DOES THAT LOOK LIKE
FOR YOU: BEFORE, DURING, AND AFTERWARD?

*Church involvement and certain social justice issues are
high-priority for me. I want my kids to see that these things
are worthy of self-sacrifice, so I model that and include them
in any appropriate way I can—engaging with homeless folks
we meet, showing hospitality to people we aren't close with,
participating in events that celebrate different cultures. I
can usually give myself a pep talk that keeps my nerves and
stress in check beforehand, and while engaged I'm just "in the
moment," but I definitely crash afterward, let the household
tasks slide for a while, and put in a movie for the kids or send
them for extra outside time. I think it's good for them to see
how I recharge when I'm depleted, too.*

DEBRA, OREGON

*I force myself to attend our local homeschool group. We are
required, as parents, to participate as well. The first year I
taught. The last two years I have done things like collecting
trash and such. I also found an empty classroom where I
could hide if necessary. I am exhausted by the time we get
home, but thankfully my husband has determined that
evening is "Mom's Night Off." Because I am organized, I am*

often commissioned for my gifting. I have learned to pick and choose, and to do it on my terms. That came after years of burnout, depression, and deteriorating health until I went to a workshop of HSPs and read the book **Boundaries**.

BECKY, OHIO

I'm married to an extrovert, and my oldest child is also an extrovert. It's important that all of our needs are met within the family, so if my alone time need has been met, I feel I have greater capacity to engage in things that are life-giving to my extroverted loved ones. Generally speaking for me, it's getting out the door that's my biggest hurdle. Most of the time, once I'm out, I'm having a good time and am glad we went. On the flip side of this though, my spouse is in tune with my "introvertedness." He knows I have a three- to four-hour timeframe before I start to mentally and emotionally check out of whatever we are doing and long to be back home in my own space.

ANNA, SOUTHEAST ASIA

I joined a group of moms to form a book club / Bible study. We meet once a week to talk about a book, talk about our struggles, and pray for one another. It's my favorite way to extrovert ever! I'm always excited to go, which is virtually unheard of for me. While I am there, I enjoy deep and meaningful connection. We often stay the entire afternoon. Afterward I am often exhausted and need to just lie down and process all the goodness in solitude.

HEATHER, ALABAMA

I am more at peace, relaxed, and happy staying at home, but sometimes I need to become extroverted to explore and learn from other people. Thank God there are people who accept me for who I am.

ANALIZA, PHILIPPINES

PART 3

a better guide

———◦◦◦◦◦◦——

*We have all a better guide in ourselves, if we
would attend to it, than any other person can be.*

JANE AUSTEN, *MANSFIELD PARK*

CHAPTER 7

always good company

*ON GOOD BOOKS AND
GOOD FRIENDS*

*"Books are always good company if you have the
right sort. Let me pick out some for you." And
Mrs. Jo made a bee-line to the well-laden shelves,
which were the joy of her heart and the comfort of
her life.*

LOUISA MAY ALCOTT, *Jo's Boys*

I *need HELP,"* I sobbed into the phone.

"You mean psychological help or just physical help?"
Rebecca asked.

I meant physical help, but I could understand why she was

confused. And I probably could have used a bit of both. As a fellow introverted mother, you know it must have been bad if I willingly picked up a telephone and ugly cried into it. Yeah, it was that bad.

Steve had been away for several days, leaving me on full-time duty with my five-, four-, and three-year-olds—one child working through attachment issues, all three with preschool attention spans and emotional capacities. Each morning I rose bravely, speaking out Bible verses and every affirmation I could muster. Each night I crawled under the covers, fatigue in my bones, trying to banish the thought that another rinse-and-repeat day would soon approach.

Usually I have to gear up to expose my vulnerabilities, even with a trusted friend. But on the day in question, I reached a sinking moment that busted through all my reserve. In desperation I called Rebecca and uttered my crazed plea for help. I don't even know what I hoped for. She had two littles of her own, and though I dreamed of a miracle, I knew she couldn't come to my rescue.

"Let me call you back in just a minute," she said.

I hung up and wiped the snot off my face.

When the phone rang, I answered only to hear unexpected mercy delivered via Rebecca's voice on the line: "I'm coming over to spend the day," she said. "Jeff will stay here with our kids."

More than ten years later, the memory still brings tears to my eyes. You know how Christians are supposed to be Jesus's hands in the world? In that moment, I felt the Savior wrapping his arms around me.

As soon as Rebecca stepped through the front door, my load lightened. A new person in the house distracted the kids, and with a friend by my side I could laugh at their silliness instead of crying. We completed the same activities I would have done if I had been alone: made the meals, went to the library—emerging with a tower of picture books, played outside, and even drove through Starbucks for two grande Frappucinos. (This was before the kids had ever tasted one, so we actually got away with that!) Later, while the children watched a video, we chatted about the highs and lows of parenting. I gushed out my gratitude again and again.

I remember thinking that the help I received would not have come, though, if I hadn't been willing to invite someone into my weakness. I had no way of knowing, however, that God planned to use that day in Rebecca's life as well.

BONDED THROUGH BOOKS: THE INTROVERTED MOM'S SHORTCUT TO FRIENDSHIP

Several years passed. Rebecca's family moved to another state; we moved to a different city. Then right before my book *Give Your Child the World: Raising Globally Minded Kids One Book at a Time* released, I got a note from her that floored me:

> The day you asked if I could come help you was such a gift. We took your kids to the library. I had never connected with reading as a child and had never even thought of going to a library with my children. Being there with you opened up a new world. I don't mean to be dramatic, but it's a gift I would not have received if you hadn't been vulnerable. My oldest will read in bed for hours, and his reading scores are off the charts; it's a natural love and gifting that would not have

been fostered at home if his mom's friend had not shown her the joy of reading with children. I began to love it, too. The Chronicles of Narnia are by far my favorite, but there have been so many good ones. Thank you for inviting me into your difficult day.

To know that God used my brokenness to bring two of my favorite things—friends and books—together takes my breath away. He really does redeem our hard places, and every once in a while, we get a glimpse of the redemption process in real time. As introverted women, we often find ourselves drawn to deep ideas and thoughts, which means we often find ourselves drawn to books. Can you remember the first title you ever got sucked into, either as a child or an adult? Maybe something a teacher read aloud, maybe a book you stumbled upon in a library, maybe one a friend recommended?

My love of reading stemmed from my love of television. Yes, really! A child of the '80s through and through, I might never have become a lifelong reader if it wasn't for PBS shows like *Reading Rainbow*. I also discovered many of the classics through movies I watched with my introverted dad. When I found out some of them came from books, I wanted to read them in order to compare the two versions. Many of my favorites included characters with vivid imaginations who also felt a little out of place in their worlds, like Dorothy in Oz and Charlie in his chocolate factory. My sixth and seventh grade years were two of my happiest, mainly because I had friends who shared a mutual love for the same authors.

The best books connect us with others. Great friends can lead us to great books, and great books can lead us to great friends. It's the perfect introverted mom cycle, a secret technique to locating kindred spirits. Why does this work? Well, often, as introverts we desire meaningful discussion. Superficial conversation just doesn't cut it. Some of my closest friendships with other introverts developed through chats about books. Like my friendship with Carrie, whom I first met at church. As we shook hands, she mentioned that she taught English at a nearby school, and my fellow book-lover alarm began to mentally sound! Decades later, we've bonded over many titles and regularly send messages across the miles to share and discuss what we're reading.

Kelly and I met when I posted in an online forum, searching for someone locally who followed a similar educational philosophy. We brought our kids and met at a park, where we talked about the books that had inspired our homeschooling journeys while the children played. We've been meeting up regularly for years now.

Jill and I found each other through a group of individuals interested in adoption. One night when the group was unexpectedly canceled, we went to a coffee shop to hang out, and the talk led to—you guessed it—books. As we swapped parenting book recommendations, I asked if she read much fiction. When she said no, I let her borrow a copy of one of my faves, *Jane Eyre*. It's always a little risky to share a title you adore with a new friend, so a few weeks later I nervously asked what she thought.

"Jamie, I couldn't get anything done!" she said. "Every night I stayed up late, desperate to find out what would happen next." We've had many similar conversations since then. So forget the small talk and go straight for the book talk. It's an introverted mom's shortcut to friendship. You're welcome.

USING GREAT BOOKS TO RAISE GREAT KIDS

Not only can books lead us to friends, but books can actually *become* friends. Have you ever identified with a character so much, or reread a favorite title so often, that you felt like you knew the person and they knew you, too? Certain characters and authors, like the ones highlighted in this book, have come along at just the right time and mentored me. They've shown me what kind of mother I want to be (and don't want to be—here's looking at you, Mrs. Bennett), inspired me, and have even warned me, letting me watch poor choices play out without having to experience the negative consequences myself.

Little Men, the sequel to *Little Women*, influenced our family culture and educational philosophy, and offered me valuable insights about loving and mentoring children as they work through trauma. The aforementioned *Jane Eyre* by Charlotte Bronte came along right when I needed to understand myself as an introverted mom. Jane, clearly both an introvert and a highly sensitive person, shows immense strength in the novel as she overcomes one challenge after another in spite of a difficult and sorrow-filled past. This helped me to accept my own personality and to see myself as a powerful woman like Jane.

Books have also helped me raise my children, and I don't mean parenting books, which sometimes confuse more than they encourage. Reading is one of the best tools introverted moms have in our toolboxes. It offers us a simple way to bond with our babes, not only when they're little, but all the way through their teens. As an added bonus, it sometimes keeps them quiet— hallelujah!—for ten whole minutes or occasionally even fifteen. Reading aloud knits hearts together like nothing else. Read titles you know your kids will enjoy; read what you enjoy; read to teach lessons without lectures. Read when they love it; read when they hate it. Read while eating or use audiobooks in the car. It doesn't matter when or where, and it doesn't have to be every day. Even a few minutes at a time starts to build lifelong memories.

If you don't know where to begin, check out a guide like *Honey for a Child's Heart*, *The Read Aloud Family*, or my own *Give Your Child the World*. Many of the titles recommended in the latter helped our family fall in love with new parts of the globe, kindling passions for countries and even history in a way I never imagined. Through read-alouds like *Number the Stars*, *Snow Treasure*, and *When Hitler Stole Pink Rabbit*, my kids developed a strong interest in World War II, one that remains years later as they've become teenagers. The love of a good book is contagious in the best of ways, even when it doesn't always look like it at first. I have proof.

I've introduced each of the introverted writers highlighted in this book to my children. Not because some expert advised me to, but just because I couldn't help myself. I naturally share my favorite things with them: ice cream, Jesus, Anne Shirley, *Pride and Prejudice*. Priorities, right? We pass on what we love to those we love, but we do so with no guarantees that they will love it too. Some people prefer frozen yogurt to ice cream, some choose not to follow Jesus, and some just don't think Mr. Darcy is cute. But every once in a while, we get a divine glimpse of our top picks adored by our top people.

For years I shared my love of *Anne of Green Gables* with my kids. I hooked them first with fun snacks combined with the 1980s miniseries I grew up with. From there we went on to read the book aloud. My two boys enjoyed it, choosing to read more of the series on their own afterward. But my daughter was not a fan. Over time, I let go of any hope that Trishna might grow to love Anne the way I had at her age.

But then the unexpected happened. A few years later I began listening to a newly released audio version of the book whenever we were out in our van, telling the kids it was for me, not them (a covert mama reading tip that works!). The hysterical narration by Rachel McAdams made all of us laugh. Weeks later, Trishna asked if she could read more of the series on audio, letting me know how much she had enjoyed listening to "my" book. Keeping my face completely neutral, even as my heart cheered, I calmly replied, "Sure, I'd be happy to get those if *you* want them." Since then she's devoured all eight books of the series, something I never expected.

I agree with my friend Sarah Mackenzie, creator of the *Read-Aloud Revival* podcast and author of *The Read Aloud Family*, who affirms that "the stories we read together act as a bridge when we can't seem to find another way to connect. They are our currency, our language, our family culture. The words and stories we share become a part of our family identity."[1] So keep reading what inspires you as well as what inspires them; you never know where it will lead.

On Having Sense and Sensibility: Lessons from Jane Austen

> *I wish, as well as everybody else, to be perfectly happy; but like everybody else, it must be in my own way.*
>
> Sense and Sensibility

Unlike the other authors mentioned within these pages, I only discovered Jane Austen as an adult. Her hilarious insights into human relationships and compelling love stories drew me in as a young mom in need of a break. But it wasn't until much later that I fully understood how much personality influenced both the writing of her work and the characters within it.

Nearly a decade later, as I read the Bible aloud to my older tweens one day, we reached an Old Testament passage that got us chatting about the rights withheld from women at the time, including the fact that they couldn't inherit property. Guess where this rabbit trail took us? To Jane Austen. I described her humor as well as her social commentary, and when I showed them a movie clip of awkward Mr. Collins from *Pride and Prejudice*, they begged for more. That conversation led us to the six-hour BBC miniseries, which then led one of my sons to the full novel and my daughter to the stunning audio version narrated by Rosamund Pike. But why, exactly, have Austen's stories endured? Why do they appeal to so many, and what can they teach us as introverts?

Jane Austen (1775–1817) grew up in the tiny village of Steventon in southern England. Her world, made naturally small by the time and place in which she lived, shrunk further because of her gender. Her brothers went off to college and ventured overseas, but aside from a brief time with a caretaker as an infant and a short stint later at a boarding school, Jane spent her childhood at home, an introvert surrounded by "good company," the kind we're focused on in this chapter: books and friends. Reading filled much of her days, as nothing from her clergyman father's large library was off-limits. The ideas she discovered there sparked her own creativity and writing projects. Her older sister Cassandra served as confidante and best friend, and the house overflowed with the bustling activity of Mr. Austen's at-home school for boys. As Jane got older, she loved watching and participating in the plays her brothers occasionally put on at home. And don't forget the dancing and country balls, which figured both in her novels and in her life.

> *It is your turn to say something now, Mr. Darcy.*
> *I talked about the dance, and you ought to make*
> *some kind of remark on the size of the room, or the*
> *number of couples.*

PRIDE AND PREJUDICE

Jane actively participated in her community, exploring it to the fullest as well as laughing at it behind closed doors. But as with many introverts, she didn't always fit in. After Jane's death, her niece Fanny observed that Aunt Jane was "not so refined as she ought to have been from her talent." Another niece, Anna, suggested that jealousy might have been to blame for why certain extended family members didn't care for her: "A little talent went a long way . . . and much must have gone a long way too far."[2]

It is thought that Jane Austen may fit into the Myers-Briggs type indicator as an INTJ—the introverted type considered "The Architect: an imaginative and strategic thinker, with a plan for everything."[3] The "T" in that stack of letters stands for Thinking, as opposed to "F" for Feeling, which describes the other three introverted authors mentioned in this book. This doesn't mean that Jane lacked strong emotions, however. It has more to say about how she made decisions, leaning toward objective principles and facts over personal concerns and sentiments. This distinction helps us understand Jane's writing, her satirical sense of humor, and the fun she sometimes poked at her more emotional characters.

And sometimes I have kept my feelings to myself,
because I could find no language to describe them in.

SENSE AND SENSIBILITY

Whether she consciously intended to or not, Jane wove introversion into much of her work. This has even been documented in a study by McGill University in Montreal, the results of which were outlined in a blog post entitled "Why Are Jane Austen's Novels So Popular? Her Characters Are Introverts." After examining over six hundred novels, researcher Andrew Piper discovered that "one of the unique contributions that women writers make in the novel's rise in the 19th century is the development of uniquely introverted characters." And surprise, surprise—Austen's novels lead the way in this trend. Piper goes on to explain, "this means . . . her protagonists tend to spend considerably more time thinking or observing rather than talking or interacting with others."[4] Whether this is due to the limited opportunities available to women at the time or a point Austen was intentionally making about the inner depth of her characters, we get to decide for ourselves.

I was quiet, but I was not blind.

MANSFIELD PARK

Publishers first printed Jane's books without any name attached, the author simply described as "A Lady." Only after her sad death at age forty-one did her older brother Henry pen a biographical note to readers crediting Jane as the writer. Since that time her influence has slowly and steadily grown. As John Mullen, a professor of Modern English Literature at University College London, has explained, "there was absolutely no reason for her to become famous—except from the fact she's a genius."[5] Scholars and flocks of new fans alike continue to discover that genius for themselves. As for me, I agree with Jane that "if a book is well written, I always find it too short." And the world agrees that all of Austen's books, as well as her life, fit into this "over-too-soon" category.

INTROVERTED MOM TAKEAWAYS FROM JANE AUSTEN

Don't take life too seriously.

In her novels and surviving letters, Jane's humor comes through loud and clear, even on the most serious of topics. This is a reminder I regularly need as an introverted mom in the thick of life at home—to just lighten up. Funny movies and laugh-out-loud video clips help me with this!

"There is nothing like staying home for real comfort."

These words, spoken ironically by Mrs. Elton in *Emma*, represent the cry of every introverted heart! So much of Austen's writing discusses the importance of home and how frail life becomes when we think we might lose ours.

Books enlarge our imagination, thereby enlarging our world.

This goes for moms *and* kids! Jane's earthly corner may have been small by modern-day standards, but the world of her imagination was not. Let's remember this during the years we spend caring for littles, allowing books to take us places we might never visit otherwise.

Suspend judgment.

Austen's novels remind us to pause before we pass judgment, to look beyond the superficial and surface level. Situations and people are not always as they first appear. I find this helpful to keep in mind when it comes to my children's behavior and my attitude toward them as well.

We might never know our full impact on the world, but that doesn't mean we haven't made one.

Mothers need to carry this beautiful truth as we go about the ordinary details of our ordinary lives. Jane's short life was unremarkable on the surface, yet her impact has continued.

WANT TO LEARN MORE ABOUT JANE? CHECK OUT:

- Her most popular / well-known piece: *Pride and Prejudice* (published in 1813, when she was thirty-seven)
- The first full-length work she published: *Sense and Sensibility* (published in 1811, when she was thirty-five)
- Something a little different: *Lady Susan*, a novella written as a series of letters—one of the first mature pieces Jane wrote as a young adult (she was around age nineteen)
- This work about her: *Jane Austen: A Life* by Claire Tomalin

REFLECTIONS FOR INTROVERTED MOMS

Books Have Been My Counselors

They keep me company through late nights,
never too tired to answer my call.
Giving helpful guidance right when I need it,
they overflow with wisdom and experience.

They've infused joy into mundane hours,
hard seasons when I didn't know if I could go on.
Helped me forget and overcome at the same time,
taught lessons without ever scolding me.

Laura saw me through elementary school,
Maud through the fun of seventh grade,
Louisa through the sad tumults of eighth,
Jane through the crazy of early motherhood.

They inspired me to dream of writing,
to dare imagine someone to love.
Books showed value in being different,
understood me when no one else could.

When I left home, married, crossed oceans,
I packed two suitcases to take along.
Filling one with treasured paperbacks,
I brought friends by my side into great unknowns.

Today I see them on the shelf still:
a welcome, a reminder, a coming home.
They have a life all their own, of course,
but reveal something of mine as well.

On other shelves, stacked upright or shoved in,
the mountain of titles I've read to the children.
A tapestry of words woven over and around,
to keep them warm no matter where they roam.

They'll carry them on the inside,
narratives and memories deep within.
I take comfort that even when I can't go along,
books will be their counselors, too.

Each page its own story, yet forever part of ours.

Reflections from Introverted Moms

DO YOU HAVE A BOOK OR AUTHOR THAT
HAS BECOME LIKE A GOOD FRIEND AND
MENTOR TO YOU OVER THE YEARS?

*I love Frances Hodgson Burnett's writing. I feel secure
knowing I'm in for a peaceful read.*

RACHEL, ALABAMA

Most people only know of A Wrinkle in Time, *but Madeleine L'Engle is definitely my favorite author. I have read the majority of her books. Forty-five of them are sitting on my shelf. I love her fiction and nonfiction as well as her children's and adult books. She once said that she refused to replace difficult words with easier ones in her children's books. She would rather her readers learn a new word than dumb it down. I respect that. She was an introvert too!*

AMY, FLORIDA

I have turned to Sally Clarkson's books so often for encouragement as a mother, and to Jane Austen as a hiding place when life is overwhelming. I have also drawn a lot of comfort from reading aloud to my children. We went through a very difficult time, and sitting on the couch cuddling a child and reading was soothing to me, whilst they also received from me when I had no emotional / mental energy to give out of my own. We read The Railway Children *and the Little House books in this period.*

EMMA, SCOTLAND

*My favorite author for years now has been Emily P. Freeman. I feel like she looks straight into the heart of me. Her books (*Grace for the Good Girl, Simply Tuesday, *and* A Million Little Ways*) have given me life! I had been trying for so long to be the overachieving extrovert I thought God wanted me to be, but through Emily's encouragement, I stopped trying to fake being someone I'm not, slowly began to* *accept who I really am, and now I find joy and worship daily in simply being true to how God made me.*

AMBER, FLORIDA

Elizabeth Goudge is my favorite author of all time. I have every one of her books, many of which are now out of print. Here is her philosophy: "As this world becomes increasingly ugly, callous and materialistic it needs to be reminded that the old fairy stories are rooted in truth, that imagination is of value, that happy endings do, in fact, occur, and that the blue spring mist that makes an ugly street look beautiful is just as real a thing as the street itself."

CAROLE, OKLAHOMA

I would say Jan Karon. Her Mitford series has been such a gentle read and a powerful encouragement in my faith. I have read all her books . . . eight times? More? It's like coming home. I love the humor she weaves through them, the friendship, the ministry. Her stories and characters go against the grain of the world: the hurried, loud, shocking grain of the world. I'm glad you asked! I never put this in words. I think I may have to pull them back out again.

SARA, NORTH CAROLINA

CHAPTER 8

feel a prayer

ON CONNECTING WITH GOD AS AN INTROVERT

Why must people kneel down to pray? If I really wanted to pray I'll tell you what I'd do. I'd go out into a great big field all alone or in the deep, deep woods and I'd look up into the sky—up—up—up— into that lovely blue sky that looks as if there was no end to its blueness. And then I'd just feel a prayer.

L. M. MONTGOMERY, *ANNE OF GREEN GABLES*

Have you ever made a commitment to give your life to Jesus Christ?"

"I don't think that's any of your business."

She was right. It wasn't.

Let me back up. As a teenager I dreamed of serving God as

a missionary full-time. I longed to make a difference, to live out my faith in a way that clearly demonstrated Christ's love. When I was fourteen, I had the opportunity to do so short-term—a chance to travel on my first airplane, to the Caribbean, for ten nights over Christmas break. Before you picture me sipping cold drinks beside the beach, however, let me assure you it was not that kind of getaway. We stayed in cabins with concrete floors and metal roofs, and I remember someone warning me to avoid the large, poisonous caterpillars that occasionally crossed the floor.

My church had connections with the organization leading the trip, but it was not directly involved—meaning I signed up knowing absolutely no one and flew down to join them alone. When all the participants arrived, we rehearsed a play that explained the gospel story to those who might not have heard it before. I loved the long hours of hard work and the people I met. But I quickly caught on that we had one main goal: numbers. It was all about getting someone to make a commitment, to pray and declare that they had "given their life to Jesus." The more, the merrier. The higher the number of conversions, the greater the impact we had made. As the days went by, the total number rose higher. Forget that I felt icky asking this personal question of total strangers; I learned to identify that feeling as fear that wanted to keep me from being courageous in my faith.

This brings me to the airplane ride home and the conversation that still haunts me, though it happened almost thirty years ago. Our leaders challenged us before the trip ended to continue our newfound boldness as we readjusted to normal teenage life, and here I had my first chance to prove it. I sat beside a friendly lady in her thirties, who asked why I had been traveling. I explained, and she responded with genuine interest as I described our group. I knew, from my evangelism training, that this was my moment of opportunity, so I took a deep breath, ignored my inner feelings again, and asked *the question*: "Have you ever made a commitment to give your life to Jesus Christ?"

"I don't think that's any of your business."

Cue awkward silence, two uncomfortable individuals, and at least one introvert wanting to burst into tears. I didn't do Jesus any favors that day. Quite the opposite. And I have come to view that conversation differently now that so much time has passed. I see the pressure I felt to prove I was a "good" Christian, a bold (i.e. extroverted) disciple. I see a teen's immaturity and willingness to believe someone else's teaching, without trusting that I could hear from God on my own. And I see an introvert not accepting her nature as a gift, viewing it instead as a weakness to barrel through and plow over.

But most of all I regret the impact I might have had on the way this woman views the unconditional love of Christ. All of this flooded back when I read these words from Jen Hatmaker in her book *Of Mess and Moxie*: "People may hate us because of Jesus, but they should never hate Jesus because of us."[1] Ouch. I still pray for the woman I met that day. I pray that God's love reached her in a more authentic way, and that her heart remained open in spite of my abrupt and inappropriate zeal.

WALKING THE ROAD OF FAITH AS AN INTROVERT

Evangelicalism has taken the Extrovert Ideal to its logical extreme . . . If you don't love Jesus out loud, then it must not be real love. It's not enough to forge

*your own spiritual connection to the divine; it must
be displayed publicly.*

SUSAN CAIN, *QUIET*

We sat having breakfast, the morning sun dancing in white streaks across the table. As I read to the kids from a devotional, one passage brought a personal experience to mind. So while they finished their cornflakes, I shared how our family discovered one of the homes we used to live in, a miraculous account you'll read about in chapter 10. I watched their eyes grow wide as I described how we found that home, how we nearly lost that home, and how God came through—details that they were too young to fully understand at the time. Now I saw their faith deepen as they grasped how God had taken such good care of us.

You see, since that airplane flight decades ago, I've touched on a way to share my faith that comes more naturally to me as an introvert: stories. As moms, the stories we share most often tend to be those we tell our children, a powerful opportunity to invest into their hearts and minds before they leave our homes.

Stories change lives, and we all have them. Many of us can trace a pivotal life transformation back to the moment of reading one on the page, seeing one on the screen, or hearing one in someone's life. And listening to someone's story is usually non-threatening. If I share how Jesus has changed my life, how our faith led us to adoption, or how God has helped me overcome obstacles, it doesn't put anyone on the spot. It's just my story.

As introverts, faithfully living out our life story day by day gives us the chance to abide by the phrase often attributed to St. Francis of Assisi: "Preach the gospel always, and if necessary, use words." Our stories also allow us to follow Peter's advice to "worship Christ as Lord of your life. And if someone asks about your hope as a believer, always be ready to explain it. But do this in a gentle and respectful way. Keep your conscience clear" (1 Peter 3:15–16 NLT).

There's a difference, I've found, between being pressured to share my faith and being *led* to share it. And it turns out that difference makes all the difference. When the Holy Spirit directs our steps, guilt and condemnation are not in the driver's seat. We may behave more boldly than usual, but it still feels natural.

One Sunday, toward the end of a church service, I saw a woman across the sanctuary quietly sobbing. No one else appeared to notice, but my heart's lens zoomed in on her alone. After the closing song, without a moment's hesitation, something propelled me out of my seat, and I found myself heading toward this complete stranger. I asked if I could give her a hug, and she said yes. I reminded her of God's love for her, told her I would keep her in my prayers. Another time, at a playgroup with my young children years ago, a mom from China whom I'd never met asked me to tell her about my Christian faith, genuinely wanting to hear how God had grown our multiethnic family.

Recent studies estimate that one-third to one-half of individuals are introverts. And according to the 2014 census, over 45 million mothers live in the United States. This means there are somewhere between 14 and 22 million introverted mothers in the US alone, many more millions worldwide. It's more important than ever that we display our faith in a way that demonstrates Christianity's relevance to them. As Adam S. McHugh, author of *Introverts in the Church*, points out,

Theological cornerstones of evangelical churches—like the accessibility of a personal, relational God, the authority and inspiration of Scripture, and the command to share the gospel and make new disciples—are paramount, indispensable values. Yet our methods for expressing those values are often tilted toward extroversion, and when we conflate our values with our methods we run the risk of alienating introverts.[2]

As introverts, we may connect with God more when we're alone than when we're surrounded by others. The command to "pray without ceasing" found in 1 Thessalonians 5:17 (KJV) may come more innately to us. And we may be more likely to agree with Anne's preference to venture into a field and *feel* a prayer rather than spontaneously speak one aloud. We also might long for a quiet, reverent style of worship service because, in Adam McHugh's words, "When introverts go to church, we crave sanctuary in every sense of the word, as we flee from the disorienting distractions of twenty-first-century life. We desire to escape from superficial relationships, trivial communications and the constant noise that pervade our world, and find rest in the probing depths of God's love."[3]

ON USING WORDS AS WORSHIP

It was late 2007. Trishna had joined our family just a few months earlier. I spent the hours from dawn to dusk, not to mention plenty of nighttime hours, keeping up with my four-, three-, and two-year-olds. One day Steve came to me with an idea: "Why don't you write about how you're making life work for our family and share it with other mothers?"

I stared at him for a while, then said, "Uh, I'm a bit busy at the moment," a hefty dose of sarcasm in my tone. I went on to explain that maybe I could write about family life at some point, but I would need a lightning bolt from heaven in order to do so at that time in my life. I did agree to pray about it, though, and basically told God the same thing I told Steve, minus the sarcasm. And that was that. Or so I thought.

A few weeks later, Steve headed out of town for work. While I was holding down the fort alone, I got an email from an out-of-town friend—a mentor we looked up to, but with whom we didn't speak regularly, so she had no clue what Steve and I had discussed. She wrote, "I had a dream last night. It seemed like it may have some significance for you. Can I call to tell you about it?"

Now, can I tell you the number of times in my life someone has had a spiritually significant dream about me and wanted to call and tell me about it? Never before that day, and never again since. When Jill called, I started to tremble as she recounted her dream:

> I saw you walking in a busy convention center. You held hands with the children, moving confidently through the crowd. Under your arm, you carried a light, a ceiling light fixture. Photos of you and the children, smiling and doing the activities of life together, covered the stained-glass dome. When people asked you about it you said, "I believe this is going to shine light in many homes."

That's how I became a writer. God's lightning bolt gave me the strength I needed (though I still felt scared, mind you) to use my words as worship, to share my brokenness and hope with other moms who, like me, need daily encouragement. At first I wrote purely out of spiritual obedience, because God was my only reader for well over a year. And while this specific story may be unique to me, my gift for words isn't. Since introverts process internally, preferring to think through what we'll say *before* we say it, we tend to use words well. These words, connecting us to God and others, may come out in journal entries, emails, speeches, songs, books, conversations, blog posts, prayers, and yep, even text messages.

I thought again of words as worship when I read the poem "Thoughts on the Works of Providence," written centuries ago in 1773:

> Arise, my soul; on wings enraptured, rise,
> To praise the Monarch of the earth and skies,
> Whose goodness and beneficence appear,
> As round its centre moves the rolling year;
> Or when the morning glows with rosy charms,
> Or the sun slumbers in the ocean's arms;
> Of light divine be a rich portion lent,
> To guide my soul and favor my intent.[4]

I stumbled upon these words while doing research for this book. I was conscious of the fact that the four introverted women writers I highlight on these pages are all white, and it was important to me to include an introverted woman of color. But if opportunities were hard to come by for white female writers, imagine how difficult women of color found it to share their ideas with the world. Yet this poem's creator, Phillis Wheatley (1753–1784), became the first published African-American female poet. Her story is one of trauma, which she somehow transmuted into creativity. Named after the ship she arrived on, Phillis came to America around age eight, a slave from West Africa. The prominent Wheatley family of Boston purchased her, later teaching her to read and write. When they observed her natural aptitude for words, they gave her an education that few females of any race received at the time, emancipating her after her first collection of poetry released to great renown.

It's impossible to know Phillis's personality with certainty. After all, wouldn't enslaved extroverts have been forced to behave in a discreet, restrained manner? However, based on surviving stories about Phillis as well as the evidence of her penchant for quiet study, it's likely she leaned toward the introverted side of the personality spectrum. One prominent scholar even called her work "contemplative and reflective rather than brilliant and shimmering," the first two adjectives having "introversion" written all over them.[5] Out of unimaginable suffering, she crafted dozens of artistic, intellectual poems that stunned readers. Phillis rarely mentions slavery in her work, but many of her poems center around death and likely reveal her pain and grief, funeral stanzas she wrote for community members who lost loved ones. Her words often point back to worship, even boldly reminding readers that those of any race would be welcome by God in heaven.[6] She revolutionized and challenged society with her desk, her pen, and her mind—an introverted world changer, indeed. To learn more about her and share her words with your kids, check out my recommendations in the notes section at the end of this book.[7]

INTRODUCTED MOMENTS IN THE BIBLE

Before we search for introverts in the Bible, it's important to keep something in mind. Clearly, no one passed out personality tests back in the day, and we must be wary of viewing the past through modern-day lenses. At the same time, we know that everyone, no matter their disposition or culture, has both introverted and extroverted tendencies that display themselves at different times. So even if we can't completely pinpoint introverts in the Bible, we can spot plenty of introverted *moments* as we seek to know and understand God better.

Let's start with introverted moments in the life of another mother, Mary, from Luke chapter 1. In her acceptance of and faith to believe all the angel tells her, we witness a scene of wondrous reflection. We watch Mary process the idea of motherhood as it's literally delivered from the hands of heaven. Later, we read that she "treasured all these things in her heart" (Luke 2:51). Haven't you ever, like Mary, had a moment flood over you as a mom, one in which you have a glimpse of the eternal, reminding you to savor its gift? Whether it's the moment we first hold our children, see their first smile, or hear them say "I love you," our hearts resonate with the divine nature of motherhood in certain instances. I first heard "I love you" as a mom at the end of a long day of potty training, and I nearly missed it. I was close to losing my remaining patience after cleaning up several accidents throughout the day. Barely keeping it together, I encouraged Jonathan to try one last time before bed. I asked God for strength while I waited to see if we'd have any success. We did, but not in the way I expected. Suddenly Jonathan jumped off, threw his arms around me, and shouted, "I love you, Mommy!" Energy and joy ran through me at his spontaneous declaration, as well as the awareness that I would have ruined the whole moment if I had lost my temper.

Of course, we can't talk about introverted moments in the Bible without bringing up Moses, who whines when God first calls him, "O Lord, I'm not very good with words. I never have been, and I'm not now, even though you have spoken to me. I get tongue-tied, and my words get tangled" (Exodus 4:10 NLT). Any introvert who has ever been put on the spot can sympathize. God promises to be with Moses, to equip him, and then sends his brother Aaron along for backup. How many times have we felt the same way as introverted mothers? Overwhelmed by what is asked of us, convinced we're not up to the many tasks and to-dos vying for our attention? This is my usual state, unless I tune into God's power. In our own strength all we seek to do is impossible, yet "with God all things are possible" (Matthew 19:26). Eventually, Moses comes into his own and fulfills his mission to free God's people from slavery.

I also love the glimpse of introversion in the well-known story of Jesus's visit to two sisters, Martha and Mary. While Mary spends her time learning from Jesus, Martha is distracted and frustrated by the logistics of the meal she's preparing—and the fact that her sister isn't helping (Luke 10:38–42). Here we see both the harried, hectic work that we as mothers connect with so deeply as well as the peace that transcends understanding in Mary's choice to sit at the Savior's feet and listen—to soak up the divine instead of choosing earthbound busyness. And Jesus honors her choice to reflect instead of rush, saying, "There is only one thing worth being concerned about. Mary has discovered it, and it will not be taken away from her" (Luke 10:42 NLT). Let's cling to this perspective when our own home fires require constant extinguishing, choosing to sit calmly with our Lord instead of frantically hurrying from task to task.

Perhaps the most beautiful introverted moments in the Bible are those we see in the life of Jesus. The son of God, he used both extroversion and introversion, blending them in perfect harmony. The needy and the curious continually sought him out, and just like us as mothers, he was often surrounded by people who wanted something from him. He knew how to serve, sacrifice, meet their needs, yet also how and when to retreat. He even had instances when he planned to spend time alone and then faced interruptions, a situation moms understand all too well. (See Matthew 14 and 26; Mark 1 and 6; Luke 6; and John 4 for more examples of introverted moments in Jesus's life.)

Watching Jesus pay attention to his introverted side is such a gift. How can we suggest that time alone is wrong when he prioritized it in a healthy way? Jesus's life on earth offers introverted mothers the best example of all: a pouring out of ourselves followed by a filling up so we can pour out again, yet never run dry. It's the recharging cycle God's own son used, therefore it's not selfish or self-seeking. Whenever you read your Bible, search for more introverted moments. Let them serve as a reminder that God created each aspect of you by intentional design.

REFLECTIONS FOR INTROVERTED MOMS

10 Ways to Avoid Awkward Church Greeting Times

The familiarity and informality of some churches in the evangelical tradition, with their best intentions of devotion and hospitality, can actually exclude intro-verts. Times of greeting and sharing in a public context, especially with strangers or distant acquaintances, are unnatural and sometimes painfully uncomfortable.

ADAM S. MCHUGH, *INTROVERTS IN THE CHURCH*

If you ever find "turn and greet those around you with the love of the Lord" moments a tad unnerving, allow this list to come to your rescue! I may (or may not) have used well over sixty percent of these techniques myself, and can therefore testify to their effectiveness.

1. WHOOPS—I'M LATE, AGAIN!

This strategy works great for missing out on the social chitchat that precedes church services. (Note: Sadly, this technique may not work for Type-A introverts who feel equally uncomfortable being late, or those like me who have extraordinarily punctual children, or those whose churches sneakily place greeting times smack in the middle of the service.)

2. WHEN YOU GOTTA GO, YOU GOTTA GO.

Not even the Lord can argue with bladders; he created them!

3. BEGIN TO BREASTFEED YOUR BABY APPROXIMATELY FIVE MINUTES BEFORE GREETING TIME.

Nobody will come anywhere near you, and they'll avoid eye contact as well.

4. IF YOU'VE NEVER BEEN SLAIN IN THE SPIRIT, NOW'S A GREAT TIME TO TRY IT OUT.

Many people find charismatic Christians extremely frightening, so you're guaranteed privacy. Also consider muttering to yourself in tongues for dramatic emphasis.

5. STRATEGICALLY SIGN UP.

Pass and collect the offering plates, join the band or choir, hide in the tech booth, distribute bulletins— whatever gives you an assigned role and eliminates awkward small talk.

6. MY GOODNESS, I'VE NEVER BEEN SO THIRSTY IN ALL MY LIFE!

This is the perfect moment to get a drink of water or take your parched child out for one. The coffee pots in the lobby are also free during this "intermission" in the service.

7. The "Where, oh where, is my pen?" or other hard-to-find object in your purse strategy.

You really need it right now! Intently dig through your bottomless purse one object at a time. (Note: To ensure success, do this with a focused facial expression, keeping your head down until greeting time has safely passed.)

8. Aha, found it!

If you still need to kill a couple of minutes, grab that pen and begin to underline or write notes and prayer requests on your church bulletin as if your life depended on it. The leaders are always begging you to devote attention to the church's current events, aren't they?

9. Walk with purpose.

Look important as you stroll vigorously down the aisle and out into the vestibule when greeting time begins. You'll give off an air that you're far too important for common chitchat and have somewhere urgent to be. Add a crying baby to make this method even more effective.

10. Use your family as a human shield.

Strategically surround yourself with them so you'll be guaranteed familiar hands to shake and hugs to give and receive. (Note: Never allow your children to grow up and leave home so that you will secure the longevity of your human shield. After all, you brought them into the world, so it's the least they can do to repay you.)

Okay, okay—I guess church services aren't all about us, are they? So let's suck it up, fellow introverts: shake those hands, say hello, chitchat with smiles on our faces. Let's also sit in the same spot every week, guaranteeing less awkward greetings as time goes by and we get to know those who sit around us. Do your best, and accept that some Sundays—well, when you gotta go, you gotta go.

Reflections from Introverted Moms

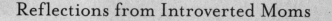

HOW DOES BEING AN INTROVERT IMPACT THE WAYS IN WHICH YOU CONNECT WITH GOD BEST?

A journal, a cup of coffee, and a more academic study of Scriptures suit my introverted learning style. I also find rest and peace in solitude and quiet to meditate and chew on the passages I'm reading (no music).

JULIE, PENNSYLVANIA

I experience the biggest shifts and "hear" better in solitude.

KRISTA, CANADA

Introverts tend to feel and see everything, and I think I feel God and see God much more in witnessing his creation. I can see God when he works together over a long period of time. I can accept quietness and stillness without being too worried. I can trust that he's doing what he's doing even if I haven't felt like I've been in communication.

KATIE, MICHIGAN

Connecting with God is a very personal thing for me. As an introvert, the less attention on me, the better. My communications with God are usually quiet and not noticeable to others around me. Much of the way I worship, through prayer and Scripture reading, is done when I'm alone, or done in my heart where no one can see. I sometimes wonder how others at church perceive me, as I sit calmly and quietly through a church lesson that may have everyone else in tears from feeling the Spirit. Oh, I'm feeling it, but those warm, fuzzy, engulfing feelings of being close to God are just happening on the inside.

AMANDA, CALIFORNIA

I connect with God when I'm in the shower! It just seems more honest that way. I am, literally, naked before him and can pour out my heart. And he speaks to me there. I've gotten answers to many questions and solutions to problems. It's a great place for intercession, too.

CAROLE, OKLAHOMA

I think there are times when being introverted makes it harder to connect with God, especially as a busy mom. When I finally get the solitary, quiet space I need, I have so much processing to do that it takes a while before my mind is clear enough to engage in prayer or any other spiritual practice. Also, in corporate settings, it takes a lot of discipline to tune out all the people around and just worship or pray.

JUDY, IDAHO

CHAPTER 9

as the years pass

ON WATCHING YOUR FAMILY GROW UP

*As the years pass, I am coming more and more
to understand that it is the common, everyday
blessings of our common everyday lives for which we
should be particularly grateful.*

LAURA INGALLS WILDER, *WRITINGS TO
YOUNG WOMEN ON WISDOM AND VIRTUE*

I don't know what's gotten into me. I just seem to want to read
all the time."

I stood in the midst of one of those magical parenting
moments. The ones that come along rarely, that you hold onto
always. And this one took me full circle, back to another world.

The spring sun blared heavy on the porch-style swing, the

same one the kids had sat on in years past, their little legs pumping hard to make it go as high as possible. Now they sat properly, feet on the ground, cups of ice cream in hand, an ironic celebration after leaving the dentist with a "no cavity" report. Several years ago, when we lived down the street, Wentworth's Homemade Ice Cream became our favorite treat spot, a family-owned establishment open year-round (except on Sundays) with a grassy area, gazebo, picnic tables, and red wooden swing in the back for warm months. I used to bring the kids to Wentworth's on special occasions or on desperate "must get out of house now" days when we needed to kill an hour and this introverted mama deserved ice cream. After receiving our orders, I'd watch my littles take turns swinging, one child pushing as another one or two went for a ride. I'd try to prevent anyone from falling off, arguing, or melting down over the size of a sibling's scoop compared to their own.

But this day I had returned with three teenagers, and the contrast startled me. Trishna and I sat together on the swing, holding our cones, as she discussed her love of reading longer and more complex books. Jonathan offered encouragement, sharing thoughts about titles he'd recently finished. Not wanting to be left out, Elijah chimed in, asking permission to read certain fantasy titles his older brother had already completed. One dozy bumblebee paced back and forth, making note of our book recommendations while keeping time with our swing. In short, it was the culmination of all I used to imagine when I had taken three rowdy preschoolers to the same spot years before.

Back then, often overcome with worry, I wondered how this experiment could ever work out. Weary to the bone, I clutched at the good moments while secretly convinced I was screwing up, so busy with daily details that I couldn't see past the all-consuming phase of raising young kids. Today, however, I can make out the distant haze of the future, its outline just visible over the horizon. A twenty dollar sugar investment at Wentworth's brought the picture a tad more into focus. I pulled out of the parking lot with a bittersweet lump in my throat, grateful for the inspiration, nostalgic over the passing of time. I now find myself clinging to memories of pudgy, ice-cream-covered cheeks even as I watch my teens take baby steps into a new world.

DECISIONS, DECISIONS: WHAT ABOUT SCHOOL AND WORK?

Small, nervous children with backpacks huddled beside equally nervous moms and dads on the corner, but my five-year-old stood at my side, watching from the upstairs window. As other families counted down to the first day of their children's school career, we made a decision that both excited and frightened me: to homeschool. Five-year-old Trishna had only been a part of our family for one year, yet it was already time to think of school. Family and unconditional love were still the most important lessons she needed to learn, so the idea of her spending more daylight hours away from us than with us didn't feel right. I also loved the freedom I imagined home education could offer. I had no idea at the time that we'd continue to do it for more than a decade. I only knew it was the next right step, one made after several public and private school visits, website research, and a ton of "Help me, Jesus" prayers.

It often goes like this, doesn't it? The early days of motherhood swim together in a blur, diaper changes and sleep deprivation scrambling our minds much like the eggs we swirl together as part of the breakfast rotation. Then suddenly, after weeks, months, or years, decisions thrust themselves upon us: Are we going back to work? What about daycare, and soon after, school? We no longer have solely ourselves to consider; now little ones will be impacted by our life choices. For introverted moms, issues like school and work can feel even more complicated to muddle through. Before we attempt to dive in, let me state outright that I do not believe there are any one-size-fits-all answers to these questions. Though I run a homeschooling blog, I don't think home education is right for every family, child, or introverted mother. The same goes for work and other big choices life throws our way.

On the surface it might seem that as an introvert, I'd be first in line to sign my kids up for traditional school. Imagine the hours of quiet! Time to get something done without distraction, to recharge with a book or a nap, to write in peace, to have tea with a friend. I could totally get into that. Traditional school can also be a good fit if both parents have outside-the-home jobs, if you have a tight community that centers around a local school, or if there's an alternative school with a philosophy your family loves. Sometimes a clearly defined split between school hours and home hours suits introverted moms best, allowing you to focus fully on your kids when they're home, knowing you have a part of the day reserved for other work.

Yet I've found that home education, or some sort of hybrid that includes it, can also work surprisingly well for introverted mothers. It allows you to design your own schedule, creating a learning routine that works for your unique family and takes into account your personal needs. You miss the daily morning rush out the door, which is stressful for everyone and can especially drain introverts. There's no homework to squeeze into busy afternoons and evenings. It's a more holistic lifestyle in many ways because of its flexibility. And don't forget the chance to avoid awkward parent / teacher conferences, fund-raisers, and the pressure to sign up for classroom duties.

What about returning to work? Some moms seem to just know what they want to do, some need time to figure it out, and some may be compelled in one direction or another based on their life situation. In my case, though I didn't plan to homeschool from the start, I did hope to stay home with my young kids. I craved the slower pace a life at home could offer and the ability to craft our family culture without dividing my energy between home and a job.

But going back to work can also be right for introverted mothers, giving them an identity outside of "Mom," providing opportunities for adult interaction in the midst of otherwise child-filled days, contributing to the family income, and, as Rebecca from California found, gently pushing you out of your comfort zone. She shared the following on social media:

I worked at least part-time until my third was born in 2015. I feel like staying home has made me more introverted, or maybe more aware of my introversion. Working pushed me out of my shell. The motivation to get up and dress professionally and engage with adults about things unrelated to my family at least a couple of times a week was good for me. I wouldn't give up the opportunity to be home with my kids, but I do see that working had some value for me, other than the paycheck.

Whether you'll thrive or not in a job has a lot to do with the type of role it is and how much control you have over your hours and position. Sign me up for mama writer any day, but make me answer phones as a receptionist, and I might just strangle you with my tightly curled telephone cord. (Wait, do they even have those anymore?) Or I might go into the bathroom once in a while to wipe away a tear and feel sorry for myself, my preferred technique during the few months I worked as a receptionist, two decades ago. This is why working from home, starting a side business, or otherwise creating your own flexible gig can be a good fit, allowing you to develop a job that fits both who you are and what your family needs. If that's not an option, look for a quiet role that connects you with others one-on-one and avoids overwhelming amounts of people time when possible.

When you finally accept that there's no guaranteed way to make important life decisions, it's both freeing and frightening. How often do I long for a proven formula instead of trusting God and having the courage to make a choice? Traditional school, alternative school, or homeschool? Stay at home, work from home, or work outside the home? Can I just let you know now, it doesn't really matter which you choose? Here's all that matters:

Paying attention.

As you make a decision and move forward, stay aware of how it's affecting everyone, including yourself. How is your family responding? What's going on beneath the surface? It isn't a mistake to try something, allow for transition time, and observe what happens. As long as you keep paying attention, you'll be fine.

Staying open to change.

No status quo, no "everyone's doing it this way," can get us where we need to be as a family. We make our best decision now, while acknowledging that seasons come and go. We have to be willing to change everything, even when it's hard—like moving from home education to traditional school (or vice versa), or moving from a job outside the home to being a stay-at-home mom (or vice versa). God might call us to face our biggest fears, to try things we never thought we'd try. And later, we may find ourselves called to change back again. It's a wild adventure. It's life as mom.

Putting relationships above our to-do lists.

Adoption taught our family this lesson early on, which has been such a gift. When you adopt, you understand that bonding is your number-one priority. Having that experience as a new mom has helped me extend it to other aspects of life as my kids get older. Whenever we press pause on our "get-it-done" lists in order to deal with a heart issue, we follow the example of Jesus himself, who always put hearts first.

ON HOW IT GETS EASIER, BUT ALSO HARDER

A herd of adorable young cousins, followed by their busy-24/7 parents, rushed past us, but Steve and I sat peacefully at the outdoor dining table with our older crew. We quietly laughed, remembering the many years when *we* were the ones up and down constantly, attending to a runny nose, administering a wipe on the toilet, or intervening in a toddler shouting match.

We recently returned from our summer trip to England, Scotland, and Ireland, the one I mentioned back in chapter 6.

While there, we caught up with Steve's siblings, all of whom have young kids. By comparison, our life with three teenagers seemed like a breeze! On the airplane journey over, they enjoyed their own movies and occupied themselves with reading, eating, and chatting. We overcame jet lag easily, since we could sleep in as needed, knowing the kids could take care of themselves. I could even announce that Mom needed a nap or an hour to work.

As my children have become older, parenting has certainly become simpler in many ways. For one thing, my kids now understand the basics of introversion and extroversion. We talk about each personality type's differences, which reflect how God created us. The physically demanding years have ended, the volume has dialed down a little, and even though we homeschool, I have more margin than ever before. Where once the daily cleaning and cooking rested mainly on my shoulders, my three teens handle laundry, meals, and chores like pros.

Yet I find these years also squeeze my introverted, highly sensitive heart in ways I didn't expect. So much seems at stake, and these days feel so important, especially since I know they will vanish in a flash. At one point the active years of motherhood stretched endlessly ahead, but presently I can glimpse the marathon's finish line. Perhaps most surprisingly, however, I realize I am no longer the one running. My new position is coach on the sidelines. It's their race from now on.

As the idea of my children branching out on their own looms ahead, I see all that we still lack, the what-ifs thrusting me back into the arms of Jesus. He reminds me what we need now is what we've needed since the beginning: love and grace. For when hormones take over and foresight is lacking. For when Mommy just can't manage another word. For when decisions about technology need to be made and boundaries must be set. For when any of us lose our temper and overreact.

The key to rocking the teen years as an introverted mother is the same as when the children were preschoolers: seek God and do the next right thing. Watching my children mature into young adults, I understand the truth of Laura Ingalls Wilder's quote at the beginning of this chapter like never before: "As the years pass, I am coming more and more to understand that it is the common, everyday blessings of our common everyday lives for which we should be particularly grateful."

These growing bodies, still seated around my breakfast table. These detailed, in-person conversations. These smiles, giggles, scowls, and even heartaches—all of which add up to equal our life, here, *together*. When my children exit this front door to go elsewhere, I want them to want to return, knowing that unconditional love awaits them. I remind myself that in the future, when I have all the quiet I could ask for, I will miss these ordinary days. And that knowledge helps me get up and once again offer my imperfect best to whatever this imperfect morning might bring.

REFLECTIONS FOR INTROVERTED MOMS

They Just Don't Do That Anymore

He used to wake me, oh so often. He'd had a bad dream, or a cough, or something felt funny inside.

I would grumble, or be patient, depending on the night
and how tired I was.
Back to his room and tuck him in.
Rinse and repeat, through many moons.
But he doesn't do that anymore.

He used to be our pickiest eater. Though we'd always
fed all three the same, he turned up his nose more
frequently.
I would grumble about this, or be patient, depending
on the day and all that had happened up until that
point.
Trying not to make it worse, we encouraged him to taste
new flavors. We also honored his preferences and
didn't force it.
Now he gobbles down chili, curry, many of his former
not-favorites.
He doesn't do that anymore.

They used to argue every day: shout, bite, whine, hit.
Clamoring for position and power, each in his or her
own way.
I would grumble about this, or be patient, depending on
the state of my heart and energy level.
These days plenty of disagreements occur, but so do
apologies, ones I don't always have to oversee or
manage.
They don't do that anymore.

The tantrums, oh dear Lord, the tantrums.

"Don't give in and they'll soon learn that tantrums
  don't work."
Ha. I never gave in, but that didn't stop these daily
  events that pushed me to my limit and beyond. For
  years.
I would grumble about this, or be patient, depending
  on how many times we'd been down this road in the
  past twenty-four hours.
At times I found myself sitting through the screaming,
  my own tears of helplessness running like rivers.
Too drained to even wipe them away. Convinced I must
  be doing everything wrong.
But they don't do that anymore.

Some mamas are reading this after multiple times up
  in the night. Or you've stumbled across these words
  soon after yet another shouting match. Or maybe
  the dinner you poured weary energy into met with a
  resounding lack of applause.
I don't want to minimize the stage you're in. Don't want
  to tell you, "Enjoy these days, they go by so fast." I'm
  not here to patronize you.
Instead let me pour a little encouragement your way:

Go ahead and grumble, or be patient. You don't have to
  handle all the issues perfectly.
Go ahead and cry, and wonder if it's even worth it.
Go ahead and pray, for strength to make it through the
  next five minutes.

Because one day, often when you least expect it, often when you've come to peace with the imperfections and decided to be happy anyway, you'll wake up, look around in amazement and realize: They just don't do that anymore.

Reflections from Introverted Moms

HOW HAVE CERTAIN LIFE DECISIONS YOU'VE MADE (TO WORK OUTSIDE THE HOME OR STAY AT HOME, WHERE YOUR KIDS GO TO SCHOOL, AND SO ON) IMPACTED YOU AS AN INTROVERT?

This past year I took a part-time job at a library, which left my introverted homeschooled son (age fourteen) by himself a good portion of the day. Although it was a positive experience in that he was forced to work independently and learned that he can do hard things, I found that working with the public for even that small amount of time drained me. And I hated not being involved with his learning because we have fun together! An opportunity arose for me to work full-time from home as a legal assistant (my background), and I jumped at the chance. All of a sudden my energy levels are back through the roof and I am excited about this next school year!

NICOLE, MISSOURI

When we moved to our new city, I needed to find work ASAP, so I decided to sell Avon. I had never done anything like that before, and the thought of knocking on strangers' doors was intimidating. But I made myself do it and discovered I actually liked it! Talking with ladies one-on-one about products we both loved was fun, and I did make a fair amount of money. It was quite an eye-opening experience. It made me braver about trying new things.

CAROLE, OKLAHOMA

I am both an introvert and a highly sensitive person. I chose my field, medical laboratory science, because I can work in a lab without interaction with patients, and work anything from full-time to once a month. Since having kids, I typically work once a week. I never thought homeschooling would be possible because I needed quiet during the day. But when my younger was in upper elementary and the older hit middle school, we decided to try. It has been the best decision! We are all able to sleep more, aren't driven by schedules that interrupt our rhythms, and everyone has their assigned work and can do it independently most of the time. That's not to say I ignore my children. But if I or my oldest (also an introvert / HSP) need a break, we are able to go elsewhere in the house.

MIA, TEXAS

I homeschooled my oldest for kindergarten. The decision was out of necessity since we lived overseas and didn't have any other option. I loved the actual teaching and found it rewarding but was left feeling like, "What am I supposed to do with her for the rest of the day?" I live in a country with no access to resources such as libraries, museums, or parks. I knew for my sanity and the sanity of my child (a high extrovert) we couldn't continue. For first grade she attended the local international school. We knew academically it wasn't strong, but still made the decision and are glad we did. We now plan to move back to the States, based largely on educational needs. She will go into second grade in public school. Sometimes I wonder what homeschooling would be like in the States, but for now, it's the best decision for our family.

ANNA, SOUTHEAST ASIA

I tried putting all four of my kids into daycare / preschool so I could work outside the home. The pace was horrible as the older kids went to one place and the younger ones to another. All the extra holiday programs and class parties were draining, and I had no freedom or choice over what the young ones learned. Finally, I decided to bring them all back to homeschool. It brought freedom to our family. Everyone's health improved, including mine. We had time to be introverted because we could determine our course.

DAWN, ILLINOIS

PART 4

simple little pleasures

————✦————

I believe the nicest and sweetest days are not those on which anything very splendid or wonderful or exciting happens but just those that bring simple little pleasures, following one another softly, like pearls slipping off a string.

L. M. MONTGOMERY, *ANNE OF AVONLEA*

CHAPTER 10

in quiet places

ON CULTIVATING CALM
WHEREVER YOU ARE

*We who live in quiet places have the opportunity to
become acquainted with ourselves, to think our own
thoughts and live our own lives in a way that is not
possible for those keeping up with the crowd.*

LAURA INGALLS WILDER,
WRITINGS FROM THE OZARKS

ou are a *horrible* mother."

Have you ever had anyone voice your greatest fear
straight to your face?

In all honesty, I'm not sure these exact words were stated
during the conversation, but those that were spoken adamantly
conveyed this tone, spirit, and underlying message. A neighbor
had overheard one of our children's tantrums, which began in

the backyard. I quickly escorted my two other kids inside, coming back to gather up the third, when I saw him standing there. The exchange that followed hurts too much to repeat, even a decade later. The cruel words implanted themselves into the most fragile parts of my heart. This took place at the same time I had started writing my first book—about motherhood, no less—and the negativity he expressed wove a blanket of doubt and insecurity around my mind. The months that followed morphed into one of my hardest life seasons.

I no longer felt at home in my home. Wishing to avoid a repeat of the awful confrontation, every loud kid noise, happy or sad, made me nervous. Each day I'd make a special trip upstairs to peek out the highest window in our two-story house, the only way I could see over our tall fence to be certain that none of our neighbors were in their yards before we ventured outside. Each day we walked to a nearby park instead of playing in our own backyard. And each day I grew more uncomfortable with the beautiful house God had given us, one I had always adored. I wished I could magically pick it up and plunk it down in the middle of nowhere, far from anyone. (Note: That's introvert escapism right there and not a healthy coping mechanism!)

To daydream away this unpleasant reality, I imagined a house that would suit our family better. We didn't need extra space inside, but I envisioned the kids stretching their legs and having more freedom to run, play, and explore outdoors. I jotted a dream list in the back of my journal. Over time, a snapshot of this fantasy home emerged on the page:

4 bedrooms
2 bathrooms

lots of character
on at least half an acre
a fence around the property
and the color? Definitely red.

Off and on, I looked at realtor and rental listings in our area (more escapism), but the search overwhelmed me. How likely was it that this house even existed near us, that we could afford it, and that the myriad of logistics required would pan out? After all, we did not *need* a new home, and wasn't this just a first-world problem, while others endured real suffering? I understood why my Nana once asked, "Don't you already have a house?" (Love and miss you, Nana!)

Months passed, and this dream house, residing on my journal's back page, began distracting me from life. I spent too long wrestling with the fact that I wanted out of my current situation, and having a physical description of another home in my mind's eye heightened those feelings. One day, while writing at our local library, I ripped out the list and threw it in the trash. I surrendered the whole situation to God and prayed that if he did have another house for us, he would bring it. I wouldn't live in this fantasy world anymore. I made the hard decision to choose forgiveness and contentment, and Steve and I discussed ways we could fix up our house by tackling projects that we had put on hold. I got out the paintbrushes, slapped a fresh color on our bedroom walls, and did my best to redirect my thoughts when dissatisfaction came knocking. I also tried, though it was difficult, to smile at my neighbor, say hello, and respect his space and privacy.

About a month later, I received a social media message out of the blue from my friend Melissa. Did I know anyone looking for a house? She and her husband needed to rent out their home in the countryside for the next two years. I asked her to send me the listing, then opened the link and stared in awe. The house that popped up on my screen had:

4 bedrooms
2 bathrooms
over two hundred years old and full of character
two acres, a child's paradise of a backyard
a traditional stone fence around the property
and the color? Red.

I burst into tears. God knew, God saw, God loved. He knew my situation, saw my hurts, loved my family and my flawed attempts at surrender. He answered a prayer that did not need answering, one that uprooted and replanted us more than seven years ago. I watched, astounded, as he brought beauty out of ashes, using this dreadful situation to unveil a new dream. I discovered that living in a rural area fit my introverted heart like a glove. Nature became therapist, nurturer, and as George Washington Carver once called it, God's broadcasting system. I could breathe again.

QUIET IN YOUR WORLD VERSUS QUIET IN YOUR MIND

Suddenly a physical margin of two acres enveloped me, and it felt like a mental margin did too. With more quiet in my outer world, I experienced an inner joy like never before. My children remained just as loud as ever, mind you, and all the other issues

I'd faced still waited in the queue. But each morning I woke up beside our massive bedroom window overlooking a grove of trees in the backyard, including the ancient maple that held the kids' beloved tree swing. Even if I'd been up with a sleepless child or knew a crazy day awaited me, that view and the answered prayer it represented calmed me. I placed my writing desk in the corner of the room so I could turn to that inspiring scene as I typed on my laptop in the mornings. We didn't have a church for a while after moving, but I spoke more to God and heard more from him in those days than I ever had.

My story isn't any kind of formula to follow, as you may neither need nor want to live in the country. Yet every introverted woman needs her own version of what I found there, a room of one's own, to borrow the phrase from Virginia Woolf. A consecrated spot, a calm corner. One of us may live in a rural area, another in a city apartment. Yet another mom resides in a crowded RV with her family, another in a self-constructed yurt on a homestead or in a white-picket-enclosed house in the suburbs. The amount of space matters little. It just matters that you have it.

And if you physically don't? Try something I learned from another introverted mama writer, Heather Bruggeman of the blog Beauty That Moves: create a soul care basket. During her Summer Soul Camp e-course, Heather guided participants through the process of setting up a mobile camp basket. That way we could take our retreat on the go, while still responding to our family's needs in the moment. I loved it! In my basket, one I rescued from the bottom of our linen closet, I placed a cloth shawl, a colorful felt bunting for decoration, my journal and pen, a candle, and a few matches. If the kids sat watching television inside, I took my soul care onto the porch. On especially harried days, I took it in the car and sat in the driveway to claim a few minutes of refuge. Other items you could include: earbuds for listening to music, favorite inspirational books, lotions or essential oil blends, a current handwork project, an old quilt. Change out your items every few months to add seasonal flair!

It's important to have your own recharging space, yet it's also true that you can get quiet in your world and still not have it in your mind. I can travel to a beach lover's paradise or take a private walk in the middle of a peaceful field, but my thoughts can still spin a mile a minute. I can unpack a basket of beauty, light a candle, then wrestle with anxiety for an hour and emerge as depleted as when I started. As John Milton truthfully noted in *Paradise Lost*, "The mind is its own place, and in itself can make a heaven of hell, a hell of heaven." Quiet without does not always equal quiet within. Why not?

The answer isn't simple. For decades I've berated myself for how challenging I find it to live in the present moment. It doesn't come naturally to silence my inner world and take in information through my senses instead, to ground myself in what's physically going on around me. Not all introverts have this in common, but I bet many of you know what I mean. Feeling as though I fail at this regularly, I often end up heaping guilt on top of my busy brain's load.

Not long ago, however, I read something that eliminated my guilt trip. An article and accompanying diagram on the blog Introvert, Dear highlighted how introverted and extroverted brains process information in different ways. While an extrovert's brain sends data via a shorter pathway, mainly through the areas that handle sensory input, an introvert's brain sends data through a much longer pathway, including the areas that deal with empathy, self-reflection, emotional meaning, speech, self-talk, ideas, expectations, evaluating outcomes, and long-term memories.[1] Whew! Are you tired yet? No wonder I can reach the dinner table and still be analyzing a conversation from breakfast! But I find this insight a one-way ticket to mental freedom. If God made our brains this way, it is not a deficiency but a beautiful reflection of his nature. We aren't overreacting or malfunctioning; we're going deeper. And we have something to offer that those who process differently cannot.

It's one thing to understand that you gravitate toward an inner world, and another to let that world run away with you. Even as I acknowledge the good that can come from my thought "fullness," I also know I can get trapped in unhealthy overthinking. I need to proactively address this, using strategies to help me stay my best so I get stuck less often. These aren't miracle cures, of course, but since we're not trying to cure ourselves from *being* ourselves, we don't need a miracle cure. A few practicalities I've found helpful: dietary supplements like Bach's Rescue Remedy and Rescue Sleep, Natural Calm magnesium citrate supplement, a lavender essential oil blend, deep-breathing techniques, a women's multivitamin (I like Vitafusion), taking a nap or a walk (both mood boosters), and using a chimes app on my phone as a signal to return to the moment.

If your thoughts have reached a dark place that you can't break out of, please don't stay there alone. Open up to a trusted friend, look for a life coach or counselor (BetterHelp.com and FaithfulCounseling.com are ideal for introverts since the therapy is online), explore medication—do whatever you need to protect and guard your mental health. You're worthy and deserving of help, not because of all the duties you perform, but simply because you're a child of God.

LIVING SLOW: LESSONS FROM LAURA INGALLS WILDER

We are so overwhelmed with things these days that our lives are all, more or less, cluttered. I believe it is this, rather than a shortness of time, that gives us that feeling of hurry and almost of helplessness.

LAURA INGALLS WILDER,
LITTLE HOUSE IN THE OZARKS, 1924

Standing in front of the replica cabin, I cried. The Big Woods of Wisconsin long gone, only a few trees still guarded the site, grass and farmland as far as I could see. For nearly a year we had planned this road trip, through Wisconsin, Minnesota, and South Dakota, after reading and discussing the *Little House* books together. The kids insisted we play the TV show's theme music as we pulled up in our rental van, then Trishna carried her set of *Little House* paper dolls inside for a visit. Alone for several minutes before any tourists arrived, we had a private moment to take it all in: the smallness of the cabin, the vastness of the land, the hard work it must have taken to survive. I looked around in awe, plenty of historical romance in my eyes.

This sense of nostalgia comes over many when they picture prairie living, ironic since it certainly didn't appear romantic to those who endured its hardships. So what, exactly, keeps drawing new generations to *Little House*? I believe it's the concept of living slow. That's what the Ingalls family embodies, and what some part of us cries out for, even as we inhabit a society drastically different from theirs.

Laura Ingalls Wilder (1867–1957) created this world that now resides in our imaginations. The second daughter born to Caroline and Charles Ingalls just after the Civil War, her family lived at the cusp of a new American Dream, part of a wave of pioneers ready to take on the world and the land. Their quest took them from Wisconsin to Kansas, back to Wisconsin, on to Iowa, then to Minnesota, and finally to South Dakota, where they settled long-term.

> It was so wonderful to be there, safe at home,
> sheltered from the winds and the cold. Laura thought
> that this must be a little like heaven, where the weary
> are at rest.

THE LONG WINTER

The family included adventure-seeking Charles (Pa), loving and orderly Caroline (Ma), prim and proper firstborn Mary, and mischievous half-pint Laura. Later two more daughters followed, Carrie and Grace, as well as a son who, sadly, passed away. In the books we get to know our young heroine as a tomboy, a nature lover, an occasional rule breaker. As Laura grows older, we glimpse a young lady with a gift for writing, a desire to learn, and an openness to try new things. We also see a grim determination to persevere through opposition and failure.

Researchers think that Laura may fit into the Myers-Briggs personality type indicator as an INFP—the introverted type referred to as the Mediator, known for being "poetic, kind, and altruistic, always eager to help a good cause."[2] I find it interesting that of the four authors we discuss in this book, Laura alone carries a "P" in her personality letter lineup. This stands for perceiving, which has to do with the way one mentally views, and practically orders, one's outer world. Someone with a Perceiving function prefers keeping their options open, going with the flow, and is usually gifted at adapting to whatever comes, all qualities that would serve a pioneer well and might also help explain why Laura waited until her retirement years to start writing.

> *The real things haven't changed. It is still best to be*
> *honest and truthful; to make the most of what we*
> *have; to be happy with simple pleasures; and have*
> *courage when things go wrong.*

WRITTEN IN A LETTER TO CHILDREN IN FEBRUARY 1947

Laura became a mother at a young age, like many women on the prairie. She married her first love, Almanzo, in South Dakota at the age of eighteen and gave birth to her daughter, Rose, a year later. Her son, born a few years afterward, died tragically in infancy. The young family of three eventually moved to Missouri, where they bought land they called Rocky Ridge Farm. Rose grew up to become a well-known writer and journalist, and at the start of the Great Depression, she encouraged her mother to write about her childhood experiences, both to earn income and give hope to those suffering through another difficult time in history. After a handful of rejections, an editor suggested that a title for eight- to twelve-year-olds might be more marketable than what she'd previously submitted. Laura went on to pen eight such novels, each more successful than the last, with the draft of a ninth published after her death. Later came the popular television show, which strayed far from the novels' story lines yet held to the same ideals and values.

Though still popular, controversy swirls around the *Little House* series. Some find it troubling that the novels are only semiautobiographical. Indeed, Laura herself once said, "All I have told is true but it is not the whole truth."[3] This never disturbed me as a reader, since the Ingallses lived in my head as a fictional family based on a real one. Next comes the suggestion that Rose wrote the *Little House* books herself, taking her mother's notes and memories, then filling in the gaps with her polished writing skills. Entire books have been created about this conspiracy theory, both for and against it. In the end, I think it likely that Rose guided her mother through the complicated world of publishing and served as her in-house editor, making suggestions and cowriting or rewriting passages when she thought she could improve them.

Of course, we must also discuss the racism toward both Native and African-Americans in certain passages of the series. At times Laura and Pa display acceptance of those who differ from them, but in other instances the novels reflect wrongly held prejudices and injustices of the period. For this reason, I wouldn't recommend handing the books over to your children, but instead reading them together, discussing excerpts as you come to them or skipping those with which you disagree.[4] I appreciate how the television series delivered Laura's ideas to a new generation, advocating for more diversity, equity, and inclusion of those with all skin colors and abilities.

Some old-fashioned things like fresh air and sunshine are hard to beat. In our mad rush for

progress and modern improvements let's be sure we
take along with us all the old-fashioned things worth
while.

A FAMILY COLLECTION

In spite of my misled, starry-eyed notions of the past, I don't want to go back to the days before indoor plumbing and modern conveniences. But I do want to see the wonder in the ordinary again. Laura understood this desire, and I long to recapture the beauty of my everyday by following her example.

INTRODUCED MOM TAKEAWAYS FROM LAURA INGALLS WILDER

Community matters.

On the prairie, you depended upon whoever lived near you, for both friendship and survival. Today we see loneliness on the rise as we've become more isolated and lack deep connections. Whether or not it's with those next door, community still matters for extroverts *and* introverts.

Work toward greater self-reliance.

Pride comes from knowing how to take care of yourself, a fact those on the frontier understood by necessity. Study gardening, sewing, candle or soap making, preserving food, chopping wood, or whatever sounds fun, then share it with your children to nurture confidence and family bonds. I am far from the crafty type, but even I made taper candles out of beeswax a few times! (Find the link to my detailed instructions in the endnotes.[5])

Appreciate small pleasures.

Those of us who've never had to go without can struggle with gratitude; it's tough to feel grateful for what we've always known. Whether it's writing in a journal or using a gratitude app, let's find a way to hold onto and count our blessings. You don't have to do this daily to reap the benefits; once a week I try to keep a journal page by my side throughout the day, writing down the good things that come across my path, large or small. It's a mood shifter!

Family lasts forever.

If you're blessed to have family, and not everyone does, pause for a moment to honor that imperfect miracle. Our family is the closest we get to the eternal this side of heaven. The Ingallses depended on each other, entertained each other, and supported each other. I pray this unconditional commitment takes root in our home, too.

An ordinary life is beautiful.

It's ironic that the Ingalls family became famous for being ordinary, for the common life thousands of others also lived at the time. We mistakenly have the idea these days that we must be more, do more, build an impressive legacy. The Ingallses lived small, yet around the world millions still long for what they represent.

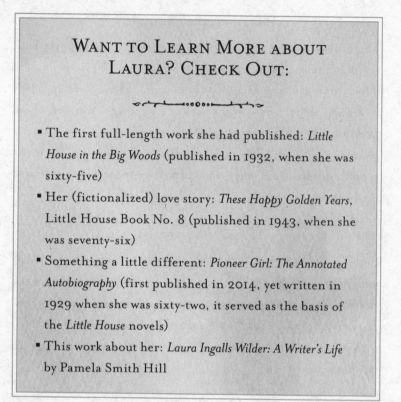

WANT TO LEARN MORE ABOUT LAURA? CHECK OUT:

- The first full-length work she had published: *Little House in the Big Woods* (published in 1932, when she was sixty-five)
- Her (fictionalized) love story: *These Happy Golden Years*, Little House Book No. 8 (published in 1943, when she was seventy-six)
- Something a little different: *Pioneer Girl: The Annotated Autobiography* (first published in 2014, yet written in 1929 when she was sixty-two, it served as the basis of the *Little House* novels)
- This work about her: *Laura Ingalls Wilder: A Writer's Life* by Pamela Smith Hill

REFLECTIONS FOR INTROVERTED MOMS

A Dishwasher's Meditation

The clear water runs over and around my hands,
pours warm from the faucet as I stand at the window.
Eager to end, I tackle the sink's pile one by one,
a needed chore to get over and done.
Then I think of those who spend hours walking for water,
those who'd marvel at this mundane miracle.
Pausing, I reconsider what my mess represents:
Abundance, family, enough.
Years ago, one of the kids scribbled in my Bible with
     a crayon.
I cried, feeling like nothing was sacred, nothing my own.
Now I wish I'd cherished the gift, written the date,
     age, smiled:
Often the things that go wrong create the best
     memories.
I hold that lesson today: not wishing my mess away,
but savoring the sacred around me.
Soon the dish pile will dwindle as young adults leave
     this home.
And ten years from now I might long for scribbles and
     dishes to wash,
which means that what I've wanted all along is right here:
my heart's desire in my own backyard. I don't want to
     lose it.[6]

Reflections from Introverted Moms

HOW DO YOU BRING MORE CALM AND QUIET INTO YOUR OUTER LIFE AND / OR YOUR INNER LIFE AS AN INTROVERTED MOM?

By refusing to participate in the outer chaos of "too much" and all the other "must-dos" that so many around us participate in. Most everyone we know is committed to something almost every night or day of the week and often eat in the car on the way to the next "thing." It's difficult to stay out of this fray since that's often the only avenue to friendships where we live, but we've found that it only leads to transactional living rather than relational living and that, too, is exhausting. We choose slow and quiet to ensure peace.

TARA, TENNESSEE

I read once that Susanna Wesley used to throw her apron over her head when the chaos around her got to be too much. So when the noise or chaos gets to me, I pull my sweatshirt or blanket or even just my hands over my face and pray. It helps to refocus me, but also alerts my kiddos that they have crossed the line in some way and need to calm down. Double win!

ANNIE, PENNSYLVANIA

Two or three times a year, I spend a day alone and (more or less) in silence. I journal, read, plan, take a walk—anything that is quiet and reflective. There is an older, retired lady in my church who is a prayer partner and mentor to me. She encourages me to do this. She also volunteers to babysit if I can't get a sitter. It has been such a beneficial time to refocus and renew my energy.

HEATHER, SINGAPORE

I purged my house of anything that didn't serve a specific purpose or make our space more beautiful. Painted our open concept a calming color. I basically reduced the visual clutter and made specific places for my eye to rest. It helped so much more than I thought it would.

SHANNON, GEORGIA

As a young single mom, I tried to keep up with my single friends. As an older single mom, I learned to take care of me and not try to keep up with my extroverted friends. I remind myself that I am a person with wants and needs that matter. I remind myself that telling my kids "no" to extracurricular activities (or limiting them to one) will not kill them. I will be a better mom without the stress of running to practices / rehearsals / recitals. Whatever relaxes me, I've learned to schedule that in like an appointment. There was a point in time when I needed a nap in the afternoons. That was the thirty minutes I allowed my kids to watch TV or use their tablets. I refused to feel guilt over that, and I was a much nicer person because of it.

KARYN, CONNECTICUT

I have realized that I don't need to apologize for my need to have "real" conversations. I tend to keep things to myself otherwise. Luckily, I'm blessed to have a husband and a few close friends who will sit down and have meaningful conversations about dreams for the future, God, politics, and insights on self-reflection. I have met myself for the first time over these last few years, and I'm thirty-five. Some people know who they are early on. I'm a late bloomer. What I'm trying to say is that when my mind and my soul are being fed, and are expanding, my outer and inner life experience a calm, quiet kind of peace unmatched by anything else I've ever known.

KRISSY, WISCONSIN

CHAPTER 11

your own happiness

ON UNCOVERING JOY

You must be the best judge of your own happiness.

JANE AUSTEN, *Emma*

Just because you *can* do something, Jamie, doesn't mean you *have* to." Mom's words rang true in my spirit, exactly what I needed to hear.

I had overextended myself. Again. Living in Washington DC, a higher education mecca, meant that nearly everyone you knew had either attended or planned to attend graduate school to get their master's. As a lifelong learner who hadn't yet found meaningful work in the world, I figured I might as well do the same. So on top of my first full-time job, I began preparing for the GRE exam and filling out applications. I studied off and on for months, then took the test. Soon an acceptance letter arrived in our mailbox. Now, I didn't know exactly what I wanted to study, but did I let that slow me down? Of course not! Instead, I barreled ahead full-steam, eventually settling on a master's in Teaching English as a Second Language. I had never, ever wanted to teach, so why I thought this made sense, I have no idea. But I think it's because they didn't offer a master's in Overnight Writing Success, a program I totally would have enrolled in.

Night classes were the only ones that fit my schedule, meaning I'd come home on the train from work, then plunge back into DC commuter traffic. Only a few weeks into this new routine, I began to suffer, and my husband would probably say he did, too! I developed aches and pains all over and felt exhausted much of the time. Yet again, it seemed as though everyone else could keep up a pace that I couldn't. But how could I abandon the program when I had worked so hard to get in?

Nearing the end of my strength, I called Mom. (It's probably clear from my stories that my telephone only gets used during negative emotional spirals!) Deep down, I wanted to quit, but I knew I could press on, do the work, manage, make it through. Mom reminded me that just because I *could* didn't mean I *should*. "There are many things you're capable of doing successfully; it's all about finding the right ones," she said.

Sweet relief flooded my mind as I finally accepted this truth. I became the happiest dropout in history, practically skipping into the registrar's office to deliver my withdrawal form. Intentionally choosing less brought back my joy and brought *me* back. Mom's lesson has come in handy repeatedly over the years, especially since I became a mother myself. I still have to tell myself that just because I can do something as a mom doesn't mean I have to. When I forget this, I crumble under pressure to grow and cook all my family's food from scratch, have a dazzling career, and make my kids' childhood idyllic. When I remember, I release the pressure and find myself one step closer to happiness.

Have you ever taken a walk with a toddler? They rarely care about the destination or about how quickly we get there, but instead exclaim over every small insect, every interesting flower (or weed) along the way. From them we learn that joy can never be rushed. It's much easier to find it in life's wide-open spaces, which is why we must protect them.

STOP TRYING TO BE HAPPY AND YOU JUST MIGHT BE HAPPIER

Eleanor Roosevelt once wrote that "happiness is not a goal; it is a by-product."[1] Although we now live in a society that makes this elusive quality its one great aim, this wasn't always the case. Throughout most of history, people viewed happiness as something they didn't have much control over. But during the seventeenth and eighteenth centuries, the idea began to circulate that anyone could walk through the doorway to happiness. They simply had to discover and unlock it. Thomas Jefferson cemented this sentiment in Western culture when he wrote in the Declaration of Independence that all men had the right to "Life, Liberty, and the pursuit of Happiness."[2] Did he understand that this pursuit could go on and on, however, and could actually detract from its desired purpose?

Not long ago, I enrolled in a free online course hosted by the University of California, Berkeley, called The Science of

Happiness. Together with thousands of participants worldwide, I spent two months delving into what brain researchers have learned about this topic and how we can implement their findings in our daily lives. One of my biggest *aha* moments happened in the very first week, when instructors described the modern-day condition they call "the unhappiness of not being happy." I recognized right away an ailment I have suffered from. They went on to explain that studies have shown those who pursue happiness relentlessly seem less able to obtain it, setting too high a standard for their emotional state, then experiencing disappointment when they don't meet that level. But those who accept their current emotions, understanding that life will inevitably have ups and downs, tend to rate themselves as happier overall.[3]

If striving after happiness tends to squash it, what have researchers found that works better? According to professors Lahnna Catalino, Sara Algoe, and Barbara Fredrickson, the answer is "prioritizing positivity." In one study they found that participants who added positive experiences to their days reported more positive emotions, more life satisfaction, and fewer depressive symptoms than those who endeavored to feel good nonstop.[4] What can we learn from this? Instead of analyzing our emotions, let's analyze our schedules. Let's build in time for the interests we know bring us to life. Not just those we do alone, but activities we do with and for others as well—because kindness also correlates strongly with a happy life. As we structure our daily rhythms around these moments, we'll begin to see happiness grow naturally.

Also, keep in mind that we often view happiness through our own cultural lens. While Asian cultures tend to value fitting in as the quality that predicts individual happiness, Western cultures tend to value standing out. But researchers have found that the following four activities improve happiness cross-culturally: exercise, sleep, growth / achievement, and social connection.[5] So if you're not sure where to start in your own pursuit, start there. Stay in bed longer (you have my permission!), go for a walk, learn something new, spend an hour with a friend. Do it all guilt-free, recognizing that "if Mama ain't happy, ain't nobody happy."

And when one or more of these activities just isn't possible? Release them guilt-free as well. You're doing the best you can. For years, I agonized over the fact that I couldn't fit much exercise into my days. When I had my first baby, I could easily put him in a stroller and get out for a walk. But when that baby turned into the curious toddler I mentioned earlier in this chapter, and when one toddler became two, I thought I'd never walk again. A quick stroll around one block could take half an hour, and nobody wanted the confines of the stroller. One day I returned home with two screamers, one under each arm, dressed in full snowsuits. They had been excited to go for a walk, then changed their minds. At least that time I did get exercise, as well as plenty of attention from passing cars—not exactly what an introverted mom longs for. I spent the rest of the day in a weary fog, thinking that my freedom as a woman had officially ended. Looking back, I wish I had cut myself some slack, appreciated how much work I was doing, honored my exhaustion, and taken more naps (because sleep also appears on the happiness list). I wish I had taken the long view, imagined the years ahead. Today it's simple to tell my kids I'm going for a walk. I can easily leave for twenty or thirty miraculous minutes. Seasons, by their very definition, don't last forever. That is the comforting nature of them.

Knowing this helps us locate happiness again, since it often brushes against our shoulder when we've stopped looking—when we can love our current season without trying to fix it, love ourselves without trying to fix ourselves, and love our children without trying to fix them. Whether we realize it or not, we are living in the midst of our happier ever after, even when our trials block it from view. Nathaniel Hawthorne once wrote, "Happiness is like a butterfly which, when pursued, is always beyond our grasp, but, if you will sit down quietly, may alight upon you." Maybe our first step should be to simply sit down.

The Daily Checklist: A Tool for Prioritizing Positivity

Day 1: Oh, the joys of a new planner. It called out to you from the aisle at Target and you *had* to bring it home. A wave of possibility breaks over you as you open the crisp, colorful cover, get out your neon gel pens, survey the blank squares. You can do anything, be anything! This time you will stick with it, work the system, not let anything distract you. Life will be amazing—starting tomorrow!

Day 2: Ready to begin—squares filled in. Meal planning schedule? Done. Daily, weekly, monthly to-do lists? Done. Chore lists for the kids? Done. You wake knowing this day is sorted. You are a victor before you've even started. You strut to the bathroom to brush your teeth, do an excellent job at that, and know you are looking in the mirror at Mom 3.0, updated and ready to take on the world.

Day 7: You're making progress, yet something keeps getting in the way: children. Just a minor inconvenience, no biggie. But while row 6A clearly states that right now you should be walking away the pounds in the living room, your youngest runs in with a raisin stuck up her nose. She blames her brother. Sigh. You take her to the bathroom, get a flashlight, pray this won't require an embarrassing ER visit. Luckily you spot it, and in a few disgusting maneuvers, it's out. You head upstairs, talk to and give consequences to brother. When you're finished, you turn off the forgotten exercise video and stare at your planning pages. You wonder how to give yourself credit for the past hour, look hopelessly at the list of missed activities, and gear yourself up to try again tomorrow.

Day 30: You forget to fill in squares after a late night of bingewatching Netflix while your husband's out of town for the week. Self-loathing calls out with each glance at the desk and planner, mocking you from the corner. At the end of the day, you fill in the empty squares with "Kept kids alive. Kept kids from killing each other. Gave them food" as your biggest accomplishments.

Day 45: You find the planner buried under a stack of paper, junk mail, and bad kids' artwork (which of course you tried to praise as though it were Van Gogh's). Oh, that's where it is! You move it to the top and make a new resolution, until later in the day when you check the mail and start a new pile.

Day 60: Your tween asks for a blank spiral notebook, as she has run out of space in her current journal. You tell her you've run out but will get more the next time you're at the store. Tears well up at this blockage to her creativity, when you suddenly spot the nearly empty planner, pull it out, and tell her it's all hers. A smile lets you know you've recovered your position as Mother of the Year.

Day 90: You wander the stationery aisles looking for spiral notebooks when you pass the newly arranged rack of fresh planners. False hope and Mommy Brain amnesia combine and rise in one glorious moment as you pull down the loveliest one and think, "It *just* might work this time."

I hate to-do lists and planners. I also love to-do lists and planners. This is not specific to all introverts, as some of us abhor structure and others crave it. I consider myself somewhere in the middle. But I'm sure I'm not the only one who has ever purchased a system sure to change my life, bought a planner or bullet journal, or created a spreadsheet—only to discover later that while the system was nice and new, I was still the same.

Why does this belong in a chapter on happiness? Well, if prioritizing positivity is the healthiest way to move toward that emotional state, we want to find a practical way to do so. There's no magic formula, of course. If you already have a planner or system that works for you as an introverted mom, one that adds to your joy instead of overwhelms you, keep it! Just consider how you can tweak it, if needed, to help you make the most of positive moments.

I have a tool that's helped me, which I call my Daily Checklist. It's a to-do list and a happiness list all in one, and it's completely customizable. It keeps my focus on the aspects of life I can control, allowing me to let go of the rest. It also helps me give myself credit for what I do, to see in black and white all that I contribute to my family, even the tasks I usually disregard because I do them so often. And it helps me remember the ways I can add to my health and happiness. The most freeing part? The goal is *not* to check off all the boxes in any given day. Instead, I recognize that each day will have its own unique needs, and if certain tasks don't get done, that's because others mattered more. Here's a peek:

Jamie's Daily Checklist

☐ Address an issue I'd rather ignore

☐ Be brave and bad (more on this in the next chapter!)

☐ Bible reading / prayer

☐ Blogging task

☐ Breakfast School with kids

☐ Natural Calm supplement (see chapter 10)

☐ Challenging conversation

☐ Church

☐ Cleaning / housework

☐ Commute to work outside home

☐ Connect with extended family

☐ Connect with a friend

☐ Cooking / food prep

☐ Discipline situation

☐ Errands

☐ Exercise

☐ Family time

☐ Get kids set up for their day

☐ Gratitude journal

☐ Homeschool research / planning

☐ Leave my phone upstairs

☐ Nap

☐ Outing

☐ Outside time

☐ Pause a sarcastic comment or complaint

☐ Personal reading

☐ Prep for next day

☐ Reading to kids

☐ Rescue Remedy

☐ Skills Learning with kids

☐ Spanish app

☐ Stay in bed for eight hours

☐ Take a photograph

☐ Take kids to lessons / activities / appointments

☐ Three deep breaths

☐ Writing time

Notice that the four happiness guideposts appear on my checklist (exercise, sleep, growth / achievement, social connection), as do the measurable activities that I find energizing and restorative. I keep my list in the Notes section of my phone, so with a tap of my finger I can mark an item completed. Each morning I highlight the entire list, click the checkbox button to erase all the boxes, and then re-click it to add empty ones in their place, making it much simpler than writing out a new list each day. A side bonus? This lets me use my phone as a tool to move toward happiness, instead of the antiquated concept of *speaking* into it, which sometimes sends introverted moms running in the opposite direction.

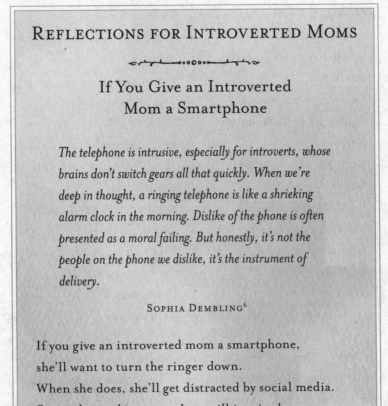

REFLECTIONS FOR INTROVERTED MOMS

If You Give an Introverted Mom a Smartphone

The telephone is intrusive, especially for introverts, whose brains don't switch gears all that quickly. When we're deep in thought, a ringing telephone is like a shrieking alarm clock in the morning. Dislike of the phone is often presented as a moral failing. But honestly, it's not the people on the phone we dislike, it's the instrument of delivery.

SOPHIA DEMBLING[6]

If you give an introverted mom a smartphone,
she'll want to turn the ringer down.
When she does, she'll get distracted by social media.
Seeing home décor snapshots will inspire her,
so she'll decide to organize the junk drawer.

She'll dump everything out and put it on the counter.

Holding each item, she'll ask herself silly questions,

like, "Does this roll of duct tape spark joy?"

While in the midst of tidying, her children will start
    to argue.

She'll reach the living room to find LEGO covering
    the floor,

her offspring waging war over the final blue brick.

The noise and clutter will overwhelm her,

so she'll need a rest.

Putting on a movie to calm the chaos,

she'll head upstairs, with a stop at the linen closet to

retrieve her hidden-from-the-family chocolate stash.

As she passes the bathroom, she'll notice how dirty
    it is.

This will remind her that the kids should pitch in more.

She'll pull her phone out, making a note to search for
    chore charts.

When she opens it, she'll see that she missed a call
    during the commotion.

Listening to voicemail, she'll hear the kids' dentist
    asking her to schedule their cleaning. This is the
    fourth time they've called.

The idea of having to talk on the phone will irritate her,

so she'll do some deep breathing.

Looking in the bathroom mirror, she will practice her
    lines a few times,

and press "call" before she can change her mind.

After speaking to the receptionist, she'll hang up,
    victorious!
And determined to look for a dentist that offers online
    scheduling.
She'll walk into the bedroom and lie down to recover,
closing her eyes for a few blissful moments.
Hearing the phone ring will wake her, so she'll roll over
    to see who it is.
And chances are, after she glances at the screen,
she will text her husband back instead of answering.

Reflections from Introverted Moms

WHAT ORGANIZATIONAL SYSTEM WORKS
WELL FOR YOU AS AN INTROVERT AND ALSO
CONTRIBUTES TO YOUR HAPPINESS?

*The main system that adds to my happiness is keeping the house
clean. If the house is a mess, then I get anxious and irritable
easily. When I go from one area of the house to another, I make
a quick scan to see what I can bring with me. I always put dishes
right in the dishwasher so there isn't a pile in the sink. I keep
wipes in both bathrooms so I can do a quick wipe down and
rarely have to deep clean. I vacuum almost every day. If those
things are done daily, then I can usually handle the rest. If those
things aren't done, then everything else starts to fall apart.*

CHRISTINE, CALIFORNIA

I function best with routine, as I like not having to think about it (schedules, housework, work in general). Most of my friends like to make lists, and they mark things off as they go. I don't like extended lists; for me, they cause stress. So how do I keep a routine and finish what needs to be done without lists? I keep an ongoing mental list of three things (and only three) in my head. If it doesn't make the list, it's not that important. Have I dropped the ball? Yes, but for me it works best. I get things done and don't have to stress about them.

LISA, TENNESSEE

I would say my main organizational / planning tools are Google Calendar and a bullet journal. I have separate calendars for my schedule, homeschool schedule, and extracurricular activities. Seeing the color-coded blocks of time really helps me see what our day / week / year is going to look like. I also have a bullet journal that is basically my "brain dump." If I can get thoughts out of my head and onto paper, then I am better able to focus on the current task at hand. The biggest key to scheduling for me as an introvert is to have one day of the week completely blank on the calendar with no outside responsibilities. If I don't have that day of margin and permission to just be at home, then I am prone to stress and anxiety.

SARAH, GEORGIA

It's majorly helpful for me to stick to my three-hour rule. When I take the kids, younger ones especially, on outings or to events, I try to be in and out within a three-hour window. After three hours, one of us is guaranteed to start falling apart, and then I feel the outing was for naught. It also helps me to keep in mind how temporary the situation is and to enjoy it while I can.

BROOKE, MOROCCO

A whiteboard has our general routine on one half, and on the other half I list specific tasks for the day. Sweet and simple.

SHANTEL, IDAHO

CHAPTER 12

a beautiful
success

ON DEFINING FOR OURSELVES
WHAT REALLY MATTERS

*Have regular hours for work and play; make each
day both useful and pleasant, and prove that you
understand the worth of time by employing it well.
Then youth will be delightful, old age will bring few
regrets, and life will become a beautiful success.*

LOUISA MAY ALCOTT,
LITTLE WOMEN

There's this . . . common path: If you're going to write . . .
a book, then you're going to write on the internet (or the
reverse), and then you're going to start speaking . . . and then,

and then, and then—and it works for a lot of people. And I think a lot of us don't even stop and ask: But does it work for me?"[1]

The answer to my prayer arrived on a dirt road, the one I walk nearly every day. I stopped and cried near the old red barn, a tiny brook trickling nearby, playing that part of the podcast over and over, slowly taking it in. As Shauna Niequist discussed her book *Present Over Perfect* with Tsh Oxenreider, she talked about the choices we make as women, the painful consequences that come when we don't choose intentionally.

My first traditionally published book had released a few months before and had exceeded the publisher's expectations. Even this modest degree of commercial success came with a learning curve, and I found myself navigating unfamiliar territory. Speaking requests began to arrive in my inbox, apparently the next step to "making it" when you're a blogger and author. I wrestled with these new opportunities, trying to figure out what to do next.

On one hand, my husband travels often for his global nonprofit work, and I couldn't imagine the two of us juggling cross-country itineraries. Also, as a highly sensitive introvert, I knew that even the best speaking trip would drain me, meaning I'd arrive home in need of recovery, even as my children needed their mother back refreshed and ready to go. So although I wanted to share the messages God's given me, these invitations didn't feel like a "definite yes."

But then I'd scroll through photos on social media of writer colleagues and friends in the midst of exciting opportunities. Envy and FOMO (Fear of Missing Out) would rear their heads as I glanced up from my phone to referee a sibling confrontation, surrounded by those who sometimes forget to fawn over my brilliance. This made me want to hop the next flight to anywhere a crowd would politely clap as I walked out on stage, but for all the wrong reasons.

I had never heard anyone else voice this struggle. Shauna's and Tsh's words gave me permission to question the traditional path of blogger, author, speaker. To define success on my own terms. And as I consulted my heart, dialing down the outside clamor and others' expectations, I thought about what my spirit longs for most:

Uninterrupted quiet to think and listen

Family

The beauty of nature

Writing

Reading

Global impact

Margin

Jesus

Making a financial contribution to our family

Giving generously

Intentional travel

Helping heal families

A strong marriage

A few close, lifelong friendships

A healthy lifestyle

Meaningful work

An atmosphere of continual growth

Using the talents God's given me

Bravely walking through the doors God opens for me

Freedom to do work I love, flexibility in my schedule, and
    finances to support this lifestyle

HOME

If someone didn't know I was an introvert, my personal success list might just tip her off. And for now? A busy speaking schedule doesn't belong there. After this realization, I replied to the invitations in my inbox with a grateful yet confident "no." But someday? I sense that response may change. Not all opportunities have to be grasped now or lost forever. They come in and out like the tides, returning when we're ready, if only we have the courage to toss them back in faith when the timing isn't right.

A "Fruit-Filled" Life: A New Definition of Success

During this process of analyzing success, I often contemplated God's perspective on the matter. I wondered how closely it would align with the world's definition of "accomplishing one's goals" or "attaining wealth, position, and honors."[2] As I looked through the Bible, I returned to an image that I believe perfectly sums it up: the fruitful life. Or to be more precise, the fruit-*filled* life:

> But what happens when we live God's way? He brings gifts into our lives, much the same way that fruit appears in an orchard—things like affection for others, exuberance about life, serenity. We develop a willingness to stick with things, a sense of compassion in the heart, and a conviction that a basic holiness permeates things and people. We find ourselves involved in loyal commitments, not needing to force our way in life, able to marshal and direct our energies wisely. Legalism is helpless in bringing this about; it only gets in the way (Gal. 5:22–23 MSG).

Here's the way you might be more used to hearing this passage: "But the Holy Spirit produces this kind of fruit in our lives: love, joy, peace, patience, kindness, goodness, faithfulness, gentleness, and self-control. There is no law against these things!" (NLT).

As we've noted before, producing fruit is the Spirit's work, not our own. Yet each day we make choices that move us toward these nine fruits or toward their opposites:

FRUIT	OPPOSITE
Love	Hate
Joy	Sadness
Peace	Fear / Worry
Patience	Frustration / Impatience
Kindness	Rudeness
Goodness	Choosing the wrong
Faithfulness	Indifference / Disloyalty
Gentleness	Harshness
Self-control	Self-indulgence

Keep in mind this isn't a divine scorecard, another way to measure ourselves based on behavior. Remember how striving backfires when it comes to our pursuit of happiness? It also backfires when it comes to accomplishing God's work in our lives. Jesus freed us from the need for self-effort. But when we find ourselves operating out of these opposites, our emotions can serve as a signal. They show us whether or not we're headed in the right direction. It no longer matters how full our to-do list is or how much we've accomplished; what matters is our approach. This brings freedom in the moment as well as when we're deciding about potential opportunities. With each new choice we can ask, "Will this move me toward the fruits or away from them?" When evaluating my speaking requests, for example, it's clear that coming home depleted would make it far more likely for me to operate out of my weaknesses; therefore, that's not the right path for me at this time.

In a typical four-season climate, no tree produces fruit year-round. Different months serve different purposes, all of them contributing to the final harvest, even when it isn't obvious. If we judge a tree during its unproductive times of year, we might decide it's dead. We might deem it a failure, make the mistake of cutting it down. If only we'd waited! Winter would end, spring would arrive, buds would appear—a preview of the tree's coming attractions. It's the same with our lives. Can we honor our personal seasons of rest, of beauty, of letting go, as much as we do those of productivity? Let's dare to define the good life for ourselves instead of swallowing the watered-down definition our world tries to convince us matters most.

BRAVE AND BAD: ON BEING A SUCCESSFUL MOTHER

Anything worth doing well is worth doing poorly at first.

SOURCE UNKNOWN

MORNING ROUTINE: THE MOM I WANT TO BE
5:30 a.m. Wake refreshed, ready to soak up needed
    introvert-refueling time, reading the Bible and
    hearing from God.

6:00 a.m. Go for an early morning run. (Do people actually *do* this?!)

6:30 a.m. Prepare and eat breakfast of organic steel-cut oats with a cup of tea and a novel.

7:00 a.m. Write for an hour.

8:00 a.m. Quick shower, ready for a day of teaching and sharing wisdom with my children, who can't wait to learn more.

8:30 a.m. Greet children with a hug and the Bible verse of the week.

MORNING ROUTINE: THE MOM I AM

5:30 a.m. Grumble while turning off alarm, recalling those ridiculous ideals I had the night before of getting up early. I was so young and full of hope then.

7:00 a.m. Roll over and look at clock on phone, cue internal guilt alarm, turn on light.

7:30 a.m. Okay, I'm up! Take phone with me to bathroom so I can "Count my steps." Text teen downstairs to request cup of tea.

7:45 a.m. Sit down at desk and log a whopping 15 minutes of writing time.

8:05 a.m. Run downstairs for a bowl of cornflakes (with my phone = more steps), eaten on the way back up (even more!).

8:15 a.m. Grab something to wear and head for a "quick shower."

8:30 a.m. Children begin knocking: "I need to brush my teeth!" Dry off quickly and throw on clothes as bickering begins.

8:35 a.m. Open bathroom door as my herd of three
stampede in; attempt to smile, but they see the truth
right away: "Uh-oh, guys. Mommy didn't sleep well
last night."

There's a big difference between the mom I want to be and
the mom I am. A big difference between the writer I want to be
and the writer I am. The wife I want to be and the wife I am. Over
the years I've realized that if I tie my value to specific outcomes
and results, I'm treading on unstable, unsustainable ground.

Outcomes often lie outside our control, and nowhere is this
as obvious as motherhood. We see it when our baby refuses to
sleep through the night, even though that parenting book promised if we just did this and this, they would. We see it when our
toddler licks the floor of the mall in front of a crowd. When the
dreams we held for years crumble or when the bills far exceed
the balance in the bank account. When our young adult makes
a life-altering mistake in spite of all the ways we've attempted
to help.

Several months ago, a podcast had scheduled me for an
interview. I hadn't recorded any interviews for a while, and I was
nervous. I worried I would say something stupid, that I wouldn't
be eloquent or inspiring. In the midst of these negative thoughts
came an epiphany: Instead of pressuring myself to record the best
podcast ever known to man, what if I judged my success purely
based on showing up? After all, doesn't it take more courage to
be brave and bad than flawless and brilliant? This new mindshift
squashed my concern. I prepared as best I could, and when I finished the call, I hung up feeling like a champion. My willingness
to try, not my perfect performance, had made it a success.

From that point on, "brave and bad" became a mantra for my family life, too. Prior to this, I would beat myself up when a conversation with my spouse or child didn't go the way I'd hoped, walking away worried that I'd said the wrong thing, didn't say enough, or said too much. Now I give myself credit for being there, for doing my best to listen and share from the heart. "Brave and bad" enables me to type these words without anxiety paralyzing me. I've taught this concept to my children as well, applauding their boldness when attempting something new. "Be brave and bad" now appears on my happiness checklist, a daily reminder of the truth Mother Teresa expressed when she said, "God does not require us to be successful, only faithful."

We can't talk about successful motherhood unless we also bring up the high expectations society places on moms. Somehow it's our responsibility to mold our kids' educations, financial futures, physical health, spiritual health, emotional health, and mental health, ensuring they thrive at all times. Viewed this way, any struggle our children have reflects poorly on us. Any immaturity signals our own weakness, not just a developmental phase for them to work through. Any public misstep is a humiliation, instead of something to giggle over behind closed doors. Any encounter with a difficult person means we neglected to protect them. Not only are we trying to do and be everything for our babes, we're more likely to be doing it alone, without the support of nearby family members or community. And let's not forget the pressure on moms to have a flourishing career in addition to all of the above.

Traveling this road leads to only one destination: Crazytown. We must barricade it off and create a detour, one that goes the scenic route and gives us permission to take life less seriously. Mothers in previous generations didn't carry these burdens; they had other concerns. A hundred years ago, moms prayed that their children would survive to adulthood, that they'd be able to feed and clothe them, that they might receive a basic education, that they'd find work. They hoped their children might not have to fight in a war, or that if they did, they would come home again. They lived by principles, modeling the value of hard work, moving toward a better life one step at a time.

Our generation is different. Many of our children have never known hunger, have never had to wear out clothing before we could afford to replace it. It's far less likely that we'll lose a child at birth, or at all, or that our child will lose us. We have machines that perform the basic work that used to take up mothers' days, but we've heaped extra expectations on ourselves to fill the gap. In doing so, our children's expectations of what we should do with and for them have risen as well.

These internal and external pressures get in the way of what our children truly need that only we can provide: our presence. Not the elimination of struggle, not a lifestyle that attempts to make up for any and every hardship. Even if we managed to eradicate difficulty from our children's lives, they'd just develop new problems to solve. There's no growth without growing pains. It's not our role to be their savior; our role is just to continually point them back to the One who is.

REFLECTIONS FOR INTROVERTED MOMS

Dear Mom of "That" Kid

*Motherhood is a choice you make every day, to put some-
one else's happiness and well-being ahead of your own,
to teach the hard lessons, to do the right thing even when
you're not sure what the right thing is . . . and to forgive
yourself, over and over again, for doing it wrong.*

DONNA BALL[3]

Dear mom of "that" kid,
You know who you are.
The other kids stay on the felt squares for story time.
    Yours scampers away.
The others try plenty of new foods. You can barely get
    yours to eat at all.
The other kids laugh at the loud birthday party. Your
    child runs and screams.
The others outgrew tantrums long ago. Yours still has
    them daily.
The other kids skip into school, while your child leaves
    marks on your hand from her death grip.
None of the other moms chat about these issues. So it
    must just be you.
That inner, insecure voice accuses and puts you on trial.
    Condemns you inside your own head.

But dearest mom of "that" kid, I have a different
    message for you:

You are valuable, vulnerable, chosen. *You can do this.*

It isn't about your successful efforts; it's about your
    faithfulness.

Whether that means doing what needs to be done or
    calling a friend in tears. Texting your husband
    a crazed "Can you come home now?" message or
    matching your child's shouts with your own in a
    desperate moment and saying sorry later.

Mom of "that" kid, there's no way you're going to get this
    right. Because there's no one way *to* get it right.

But you are going to *be* there. You are going to stay. And
    that simple act of courage will speak volumes over
    the years and decades ahead.

It's going to be okay. You're going to be okay. Your
    child's going to be okay.

Dear mom of "that" kid,

You know who you are. And I do, too.

You are: precious, freed from the need to be perfect,
    giving your personal best.

You're a wonderful mother, and I believe in you.

SENT YOUR WAY WITH LOVE FROM JAMIE,

ANOTHER MOM OF "THAT" KID

Reflections from Introverted Moms

IN THE MIDST OF A WORLD AND SOCIETY THAT
TELLS US SUCCESS SHOULD LOOK A CERTAIN
WAY, HOW DO YOU PERSONALLY DEFINE IT AS
AN INTROVERTED WOMAN AND MOM?

Success for me has been playing to my strengths and outsourcing the rest for my extroverted kids! I often read out loud during meals, not just to get good literature in, but also to quell the mealtime noise. I've been resting in the fact that my kids seem to like being with me, and I like being with them. Our family life might not look like others', but it works for us, and we are happy.

JENNIFER, ZAMBIA

With a finite amount of interacting energy, success for me is accepting my limits, wisely prioritizing who gets that energy and when. Success also looks like apologizing to others and forgiving myself when I overextend myself. Sometimes, no matter how gracefully I bow out of situations, some people are going to misunderstand and harshly judge. It is vital for me to remember that the extroverted world may not understand, but God does! We must never forget that we are fully known and fully loved.

CASEY, CALIFORNIA

It may sound like a cliché, but I would define success as inner peace that overflows to every aspect of our lives. Leaving a legacy and significance especially with your kids and people around you. To keep running the race that was set before you with gratefulness and a dreamer's heart: that sums up success for me.

LORIE, PHILIPPINES

We have to own our limitations and work within them. We have to be honest about who we are to ourselves and others. God made us this way. So he has plans to use us the way we are. We are the one-on-one folks. The ones who send a note or a text when we know you are struggling, the ones with the blogs about how it's okay not to be the perfect mom and wife. We are the encouragers and the background folks. We all have a purpose.

ANGIE, ALABAMA

Success comes when you look at each individual step you have taken out of your comfort zone. Celebrate those small steps. And when you recognise your limits too, even though these two may seem contradictory. There are times when we need to go beyond what is comfortable for us, such as advocating for our children. At the same time, knowing how to say no to things is huge, but feeling comfortable with that choice is even bigger. To me, these are successes.

MANDY, AUSTRALIA

AN INTROVERTED MOM'S MANIFESTO

Believing I am a child of God, a gift to my family and the world, and in order to nurture myself as a woman, mother, and introvert, I will:

Be true to how God created me.

I will honor my personality, knowing I am more than enough as I am. I will focus on my strengths, acknowledging the ways my introversion blesses others.

Accept and embrace my limits.

I will look for "definite yeses" and refuse to settle for less. When I say no, I'll do so without guilt. When I say yes, I'll do so with enthusiasm, acting within my sweet spot.

Nourish myself, knowing that rest makes me a better mom.

I won't sacrifice the essence of who I am on a self-made altar of perfectionism. It isn't selfish to need a break from my children. I'll choose self-care over self-improvement.

Go through difficult life seasons according to my temperament.

I won't pretend away hardship or disappointment; I will care for the little girl I once was and still am. I'll extend kindness to myself and accept it from others on behalf of the One who promises to comfort the brokenhearted.

Seek to understand my children's personalities.

If I have extroverts, I'll celebrate and nurture their exuberance. If I have introverts, I'll teach them to value their nature even as I model how I value my own.

Step out of my comfort zone when I sense it's right.

Courage isn't the absence of fear, but action in spite of it. I will be brave and bad. Following in the footsteps of introverts like Lincoln, Gandhi, and Rosa Parks, I'll remember that boldness does not reside within the realm of extroverts alone.

Make time for good books and good friends.

Whether I read a sentence, a page, or a chapter, I'll soak up inspiring words. Whether I send a quick text, meet for coffee, or get on the telephone(!), I'll invest in friendship, thereby investing in happiness.

Connect with God in ways that come naturally.

I may "feel a prayer," read or recite a line of Scripture, write in a journal. I may go to church or commune in the sanctuary of nature. I'll let my life story display the love of God.

Imagine life five or ten years from now.

When my present days seem long and loud, I'll take mental and physical snapshots of our current crazy to treasure in the future: his toothless grin, her "help" in the kitchen, chubby arms around my neck—the miracle of being the center of someone's world.

Cultivate calm in my world and my mind.

I will brew tea or coffee, step outside and exhale, wash my mug with intention, refuse to overanalyze. I'll retreat to a quiet spot, even if I'm only there two minutes before the next knock comes.

Stop striving to feel happy all the time.

I'll acknowledge life's inevitable ups and downs while prioritizing positivity in my days. When I need to, I'll leave technology in a drawer, and walk away, free.

Dare to define the good life on my own terms.

I won't measure myself based on how much I get done. I'll pay more attention to how I get it done. When I notice frustration building, I'll view my negative emotions as a caution light pointing me back toward the life I most desire.

Forgive myself.

When nothing works, when I screw up, feel drained by our schedule or emotionally exhausted from constant noise, I'll let grace cover all. I'll allow imperfection in my home, my family, and myself. I'll go to bed as soon as I can, get up, and try again. Because what my children need most from their introverted mom today and tomorrow is just for me *to be here.*

And that I promise, with love, to do.

dear fellow introverted moms

Dear fellow introverted moms,

You are my people, and I'm so glad we found each other! If I could, I would wave a magic wand over your life right now, before you close the back cover of this book. It would grant you sleep each night, quiet each afternoon, patience each morning, and the ability to skip small talk forever.

But we both know what will happen tomorrow. The issues and interruptions you dealt with before you read this book? They'll still be there. Whatever situation is pushing you beyond your limits? Still there. The character flaws you struggle with? Yep. There. (Sorry, my magic doesn't reach very far!)

My hope and prayer, though, is that one small thing is different: Now you know you're not the only one.

Please take that tiny comfort with you, wrapping it around your shoulders like a cozy fleece. Keep it tucked in your mind when you're surrounded by extroverts who appear to do more, when you crawl onto the couch for a midday reset, when that internal voice tries to "not enough" you again.

And if you'd like to journey with other like-minded women, check out our growing Introverted Moms community at IntrovertedMoms.com, where we can continue the chat and support each other in our real life here and now. You're one of us.

*Written with love, cinnamon
tea, and a dark chocolate
peanut butter cup in hand,*

Jamie

acknowledgments

I have to start by sending out thanks to the fellow introverted mothers who have read my work over the past ten years. I had no idea that what I was sharing would make sense to anyone else, but suddenly I felt less alone. I hope that's how you feel now. Thank you for helping me believe this book was needed. I also want to thank all the introverted moms who shared their thoughts and experiences on social media and allowed me to put their words here. These pages are stronger because of you.

Thank you, Jenni Burke of D.C. Jacobson, for becoming giddy over this idea with me, yet never pushing me to move too fast on it. I'm blessed to have you as both agent and friend. I'm also grateful to have had two experienced editors I trust stewarding this project through its many phases: Sandy Vander Zicht and Carolyn McCready. And thanks to Alicia Kasen, Harmony Harkema, Robin Barnett, and the rest of the hardworking team at Zondervan for guiding me along this journey.

On SimpleHomeschool.net, I'm fortunate to share virtual space with an amazing team of writers. Thank you Kara

Anderson, Kris Bales, Purva Brown, Cait Fitzpatrick Curley, Kara Fleck, Kari Patterson, Melissa Camara Wilkins, and Shawna Wingert. You kept the site going with your inspired words even as I tried to write these inspired words. You're some of the most incredible ladies I've ever known, plus you're all introverts, which gets you bonus points!

Shawna, Kari, and Jill: Thank you for being *Introverted Mom*'s very first readers. The time you invested and your comments scribbled in the margins warmed my heart and kept me going when I could no longer think straight. I am holding on to them to go back to when discouragement strikes.

Maud, Laura, Louisa, and Jane: Thank you for the decades of inspiration. I will be president of your (introverted) fan clubs forever.

Thank you to our families in both England and North Carolina! It's so good to have people you belong with and who are stuck with you forever. Love you all.

Even introverts need friends, and God has given me some of the best. Thank you Kelly Gawitt, Jill Turner, Melissa Massett, Carrie DePasquale, Rachel DePasquale, and Mirjam Picard—for inviting my family and me into your hearts and homes. You are such a gift.

Thank you, Caroline Starr Rose, for telling me when my writing is not its best, helping me make it better, and listening to me whine, cry, and laugh via Voxer, the best app ever invented for introverted friends. Thank you, Jenniffer, for being a mentor and friend to our kids. This book would not exist if it weren't for all your hard work, which gave me the hours needed to do this hard work. I'm so glad God sent you to sit in front of us at church three years ago.

Steve, twenty years later, I can say without a doubt that I'd still choose you. Thank you for loving me so well for so long. I will listen to you verbally process for all my days. Trishna, thank you for wanting to hear each chapter of this book as soon as it was completed. Jonathan, thank you for bringing me a cup of tea and a hug every morning while I wrote. Elijah, thank you for singing "I love you, Mommy, oh yes I do." I'll love you all forever; I'll like you for always. And remember: Magic always comes with a price!

God, thank you for books, chocolate, tea, family, Jesus, love. In other words, for everything.

notes

Introduction

1. For more specific information about your unique personality type, I recommend taking an online test. Find free ones at truity.com and 16personalities.com.

Chapter 1: The Distance Is Nothing

1. John Piper, *Don't Waste Your Life* (Wheaton, IL: Crossway, 2003), 33.
2. Susan Cain, *Quiet Power* (New York: Dial Books, 2016), 27.
3. Susan Storm, "How Each Myers-Briggs Type Reacts to Stress (and How to Help!)," *Psychology Junkie*, August 2, 2015, https://www.psychologyjunkie.com/2015/08/02/how-each-mbti-type-reacts-to-stress-and-how-to-help/.

Chapter 2: Learning How to Sail

1. Susan Cain, *Quiet: The Power of Introverts in a World That Can't Stop Talking* (New York: Random House, 2012), 11.
2. Ednah Cheney, *Louisa May Alcott: Her Life, Letters, and Journals* (Carlisle, MA: Applewood, 2010), 29. Other journal quotes found here as well.
3. Description found at https://www.16personalities.com/personality-types.

4. Louisa May Alcott, *Little Women*, Reprint edition (New York: Puffin, 2014), 721.

Chapter 3: A New Day

1. This is an ebook that can be found at https://www.carrotsfor michaelmas.com/good-reads/.

Chapter 4: No Great Loss

1. Kathryn Van Auken, "Grieving When You're an Introvert," Huffington Post, April 13, 2016, https://www.huffingtonpost .com/kathryn-van-auken/grieving-when-youre-an-introvert _b_9627664.html.
2. Description found at https://www.16personalities.com /personality-types.
3. Quotes from Maud's journals found in *The Selected Journals of L M. Montgomery*, Volumes One and Two, edited by Mary Rubio and Elizabeth Waterston (Ontario: Oxford University Press, 1985 and 1987).

Chapter 5: Tenderness of Heart

1. Shawna Wingert, "To the Single Mom at Christmas," Not the Former Things (blog), December 14, 2015, https://notthe formerthings.com/to-the-single-mom-on-christmas.
2. Also check out this video clip on YouTube to share with your spouse: "Introvert VS. Extrovert // Which are you?" Holderness Family Vlogs, Jan. 31, 2018, https://www.youtube.com/watch ?v=Z2R2KGW69mo.
3. Susan Cain, *Quiet: The Power of Introverts in a World That Can't Stop Talking* (New York: Random House, 2012), 264.

Chapter 6: Pruned Down and Branched Out

1. Hannah Whitall Smith, *The Christian's Secret of a Happy Life*, Reprint edition (Peabody, MA: Hendrickson, 2004), 89.
2. Greg McKeown, *Essentialism: The Disciplined Pursuit of Less* (New York: Crown Business, 2014), 103.
3. Gretchen Rubin, *The Happiness Project* (New York: HarperCollins, 2009), 11.

4. Megan M. Fritz and Sonja Lyubomirsky, "How and Why Positive Activities Can Make You Happier," *Behavioral Scientist*, March 20, 2018, http://behavioralscientist.org/how-and-why-positive-activities-can-make-you-happier/.
5. Elaine N. Aron, "The Highly Sensitive Person" *The Highly Sensitive Person*, 1999, http://www.hsperson.com/pages/hsp.htm.
6. Elaine N. Aron, *The Highly Sensitive Person: How to Thrive When the World Overwhelms You* (New York: Broadway Books), 19–20.
7. Anne Bogel, "Self-care for the Highly Sensitive Parent," *Simple Homeschool*, October 29, 2014, https://simplehomeschool.net/highly-sensitive-parent/.
8. *The Hobbit: An Unexpected Journey.* Directed by Peter Jackson, performances by Martin Freeman and Ian McKellen, New Line Cinema, 2012.

Chapter 7: Always Good Company

1. Sarah Mackenzie, *The Read Aloud Family* (Grand Rapids: Zondervan, 2018), 38.
2. Claire Tomalin, *Jane Austen: A Life* (New York: Vintage Books, 1999), 136–137.
3. "INTJ Personality: The Architect," 16 Personalities, https://www.16personalities.com/intj-personality.
4. Andrew Piper, "Why Are Jane Austen's Novels So Popular? Her Characters Are Introverts," .txtLAB, April 29, 2016, https://txtlab.org/2016/04/why-are-jane-austens-novels-so-popular-her-characters-are-introverts/.
5. Quoted by Jodie Halford in "Why Is Jane Austen Trending 200 Years after Her Death?" BBC News, July 18, 2017, http://www.bbc.com/news/uk-england-40644085.

Chapter 8: Feel a Prayer

1. Jen Hatmaker, *Of Mess and Moxie* (Nashville: Nelson Books, 2017), 79.
2. Adam S. McHugh, *Introverts in the Church* (Downers Grove, IL: InterVarsity Press, 2017), 25.
3. Ibid., 198.
4. Phillis Wheatley, "Thoughts on the Works of Providence," *The Poems of Phillis Wheatley: With Letters and a Memoir* (Mineola, NY:

Dover Publications, 2010), 19–22. Find the entire poem online at bartleby.com/150/12.html.

5. John C. Shields, "Phillis Wheatley's Use of Classicism," *American Literature* 52, no. 1 (1980), 100.

6. Phillis Wheatley, "On Being Brought from Africa to America," *The Poems of Phillis Wheatley: With Letters and a Memoir* (Mineola, NY: Dover Publications, 2010), 3. Find entire poem online at bartleby.com/150/5.html.

7. For kids ages ten and up, check out *The Poems of Phillis Wheatley: With Letters and a Memoir* (Mineola, NY: Dover Publications, 2010). For further adult study consult *Phillis Wheatley, Complete Writings* (New York: Penguin, 2001).

Chapter 10: In Quiet Places

1. Jean Granneman, "Introverts' and Extroverts' Brains Really Are Different, According to Science," Introvert, Dear (blog), March 4, 2015, https://introvertdear.com/news/introverts-and -extroverts-brains-really-are-different-according-to-science/.

2. Description of INFP found at https://www.16personalities.com /personality-types.

3. Quoted by Pamela Smith Hill, *Laura Ingalls Wilder: A Writer's Life* (Pierre: South Dakota State Historical Society Press, 2007), 1.

4. For further information, watch author Grace Lin's video on PBS.org, What to do when you realize classic books from your childhood are racist: https://www.pbs.org/newshour/show /realize-classic-books-childhood-racist.

5. Find my instructions on how to make candles with kids at https ://simplehomeschool.net/candle-making-with-kids/.

6. "If I ever go looking for my heart's desire again, I won't look any further than my own back yard. Because if it isn't there, I never really lost it to begin with." L. Frank Baum, *The Wonderful Wizard of Oz*.

Chapter 11: Your Own Happiness

1. Eleanor Roosevelt, *You Learn by Living* (New York: Harper, 1960), 95.

2. Transcription of the Declaration of Independence, *National*

Archives, https://www.archives.gov/founding-docs/declaration
-transcript.

3. Dacher Keltner and Emiliana Simon-Thomas, *The Science of
Happiness: Week 1*, Edx.org, 2018, https://courses.edx.org/courses
/coursev1:BerkeleyX+GG101x+1T2018/course/.

4. L. I Catalino, S. B. Algoe, and B. L. Fredrickson (2014).
"Prioritizing Positivity: An Effective Approach to Pursuing
Happiness?" Emotion, 14 (2014): 1155–61, http://www.unc.edu
/peplab/publications/Catalino%20Algoe%20Fredrickson%20
2014.pdf.

5. Keltner and Simon-Thomas, *The Science of Happiness: Week 1*, Edx.
org, 2018, https://courses.edx.org/courses/coursev1:BerkeleyX
+GG101x+1T2018/course/.

6. Sophia Dembling, "Nine Signs That You Might Be an Introvert,"
Huffington Post, December 7, 2012, https://www.huffingtonpost
.com/sophia-dembling/nine-signs-that-you-might_b_2251932
.html.

Chapter 12: A Beautiful Success

1. Shauna Niequist and Tsh Oxenreider, The Simple Show podcast,
Episode 38, August 27, 2016, https://theartofsimple.net/podcast
/38/.

2. Dictionary.com, https://www.dictionary.com/browse/success?s=t.

3. Donna Ball, *At Home on Ladybug Farm* (New York: Berkley, 2009),
255.